BANBURY
during the
GREAT WAR

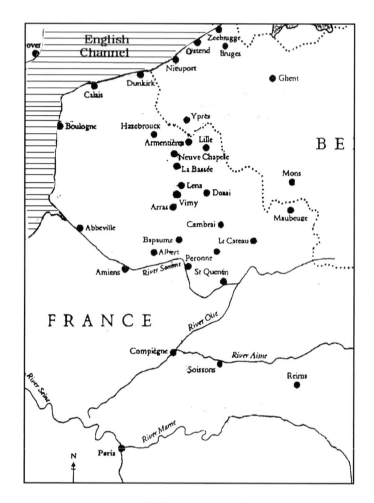

Map of the Western front

BANBURY
during the
GREAT WAR

by
Kevin Northover

 Prospero
Publications

Prospero Publications
260 Colwell Drive, Witney, Oxon, OX28 5LW

First Published 2003

© Kevin Northover and
Prospero Publications

ISBN 1 899246 50 9

Typsetting and reprographics by
Prospero Publications
Printing by Alden Press, Oxford

Introduction

I first became interested in the Great War as a young boy just over thirty years ago whilst working in my grandfather Mr Alec Batts shoe repair shop in Parsons Street. I would listen intently as he and his friends chatted about the old days and of their lost childhood friends. On occasions they gave me souveniers of the war, a medal, a badge, or maybe an ageing photograph and I soon became an avid collector.

   Photographs and documents became my main passion and I soon built up an interesting archive. Many items were connected with places and people of Banbury and years later I was determined to find out more of what was depicted in these sepia snapshots.

   Suprisingly information at the museum and library was sparse but after trawling through old newspapers and official records I began to uncover some interesting facts about Banbury's part in the conflict.

   In an old copy of the *Banbury Guardian* I read that at a meeting of the Red Cross Society at the Municipal School on January 24, 1919 the Commandant Mr S J Mawle, MBE commented that;

 'He hoped somone with literary talent would write a history of what Banbury had done in the Great War'.

   In an attempt to at least record some of this town's part in the 1914-18 war here is my offering some eighty years on.

Dedication

This book is dedicated to the memory of my grandfather, Mr Alec Batts 1901 - 1984. The inspiration of my interest in the Great War and ultimately this work. Also for my father Don Northover 1929 - 2000.

Kevin Northover
2003

Acknowledgements

Many people have assisted in the research and eventual production of this book. I am indebted to Barry Davis for the use of many photographs and items of ephemera from his personal collection. My thanks also to Chris Kelly of Banbury Museum, also Louise Liberatos and Nancy Long who have made much information available to me.

The research has taken many years to complete and the following have all assisted in some way, be it through the lending of photographs, being interviewed or searching through private or museum archives. I am very grateful to them all.

Mr G C Hartland   Mrs D Mold, nee Gasson
Mr J Coggins and family   Mr D Solomon
Mr E Lester   Mrs Woollams
Miss B Adkins   Mrs L Mold
Mrs A Tanner   Stroud family
Mrs B Pratt and residents of Levenot Close
Mrs E Shea (British Legion)   Former residents of Orchard Lodge
Mr M Allitt and Staff Banbury Centre for Local Studies
Banbury Museum   Banbury Guardian
Oxfordshire Photographic Archives
Commonwealth Wargraves Commission
Imperial War Museum   Royal Artillery Museum
Worcestershire Regimental Museum Essex Regimental Museum
Royal Green Jackets Museum
Richard Jeffs and the staff of the Regimental Archives, Oxfordshire and Buckinghamshire Light Infantry Museum
Mr Marsh and the QOOH Old Comrades

The following have given a great deal of their time and practical help in finally putting the book together. Thanks to my Mother, Jean Northover, Miss K Northover, Miss L Taylor and of course Bill Simpson for his guidance and patience.

Kevin Northover
Banbury
2003

Contents

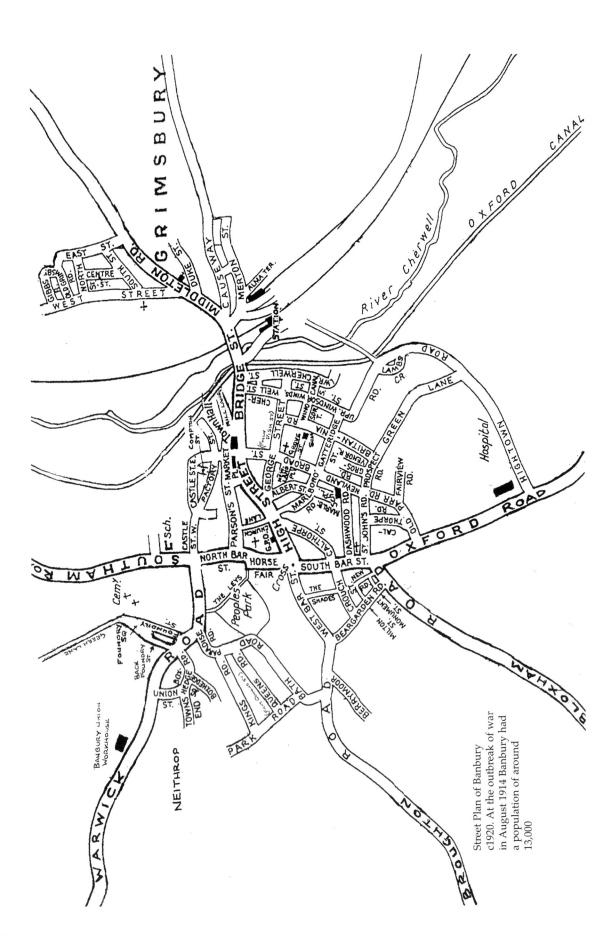

Street Plan of Banbury c1920. At the outbreak of war in August 1914 Banbury had a population of around 13,000

Oxfordshire Yeomanry parade in Horsefair, Banbury 1910 on the death of Edward VII.

Stroud Family

The War begins in Banbury

Few words were exchanged but many eyes glanced anxiously at the clock as its fingers moved inexorably towards 11 o'clock pm. It was the last summer twilight of peace for four years. His Majesty's Government had issued an ultimatum to Germany that it must promise to respect and not violate Belgium's neutrality, this ultimatum expired at that time. St Mary's Church struck the eleventh hour without word from Germany, it was war!

The Foreign Office made a declaration at 12.15 am August 5, 1914.
'Owing to the summary rejection by the German Government of the request made by His Majesty's Government for the assurance that the neutrality of Belgium would be respected, His Majesty's Ambassador in Berlin has received his passports and His Majesty's Government has declared to the German Government that a state of war exists between Great Britain and Germany from 11 pm August 4, 1914.'

The nation was stunned, at all places of worship the following Sunday prayers for peace were offered. People crowded the streets in this pre-radio age anxious for news hoping, as it transpired in vain, that some power would even now avert what must be perceived as a terrible prospect. Telegrams were posted at the Banbury Guardian's offices with the latest news.

On the following Monday midday the local Territorials returned from the

Townspeople see recruits off to Oxford in 1914 on the station approach.

Barry Davis

camp at Marlow, whither they had gone the previous day, with instructions to await mobilisation orders. The order in council calling out the Army Reserve and embodying the Territorial Force was issued during Tuesday and the copy posted at the Town Hall became another centre of interest. The anxiety of the people was such that they could not abide the isolation of their homes and continually crowded the streets. There was some rush to lay in food supplies which caused a rise in prices. Leading local provision merchants when interviewed said it was impossible to quote prices, they varied from hour to hour and had increased tremendously in two days. In the opinion of one, if the trade had charged a heavy increase on existing stocks it would have checked the panic buying which had produced the rise.

If you're - 5' 3" and fit ———.

K Northover

Recruitment

On the outbreak of the war the call went out immediately for volunteers to join the colours. Unmarried men between the ages of 18 and 30 were asked to join, terms of enlistment being three years or the duration of the war. Recruiting posters and advertisements appeared in the local newpapers to try and encourage men to sign on. The parliamentary recruiting committee instigated a campaign whereby all householders received a form to fill in with the name and age of all males between 19 and 38 living at that address who were willing to enlist for the duration of the war. This form also asked for the names of anybody serving in the forces.

The casualty lists and obituaries started to appear in the Banbury Guardian and Banbury Advertiser but people remained optimistic and there was a feeling of confidence of an early victory, few foresaw a long drawn out struggle. In Banbury as in other parts of the country feelings over recruitment ran high. Women were urged to get their menfolk into khaki and white feathers, a mark of cowardice, were handed over indiscriminately. In 1915 Hilda Stroud of

Lord North (in uniform) oversees Banbury recruits forming up prior to their departure for Oxford,
September 1914. Photograph believed to have been taken in North Bar, Horsefair area.

Banbury Museum

Grimsbury wrote to her brother George, a private in the Army Service Corps:
'Daisy and I tell them all to get into khaki now. Our poor Sydney and you had
to go and N———— B———— and R———— stayed at home, cowards thats
what I think they are!'

By mid 1915 as casualties mounted the government looked towards conscription. Their first priority was to find out about the nations manpower. On
August 15 a census was carried out, this produced a National Register of
everybody between the age of 15 and 65, name, address and occupation. Many
saw this as the first step towards compulsory service.

The voluntary recruiting system began to collapse under the demands of the
trenches and in an attempt to bolster it up , the 'Derby' scheme was introduced.
This was put into effect by Lord Derby the Director of Recruitment and it was
the basis of conscription in Britain. Before the war Britain was one of the few
continental countries not using conscription. What the 'Derby' scheme did was
adopt the continental practice of dividing all the adult males of the country
into annual classes, each class in turn became available for military service
with the changing calendar. Initially no married men were to be considered
until there were no longer any unmarried men available. There was to be no
compulsion, the scheme relied on persuasion to pressurise men into attesting,
that is to undertake if and when called upon to do so. By early 1916 the 'Derby
men' were being called, proceeding daily to their depots and then to their

C and G Company's of the 1st/4th Oxford & Bucks L I leaving Banbury Great Western Railway station for Oxford on August 5, 1914.
Richard Jeffs

Banbury volunteers for the army. The elderly gentleman in the front row is believed to be Mr Samuelson. He holds a sign that reads 'some of the Banbury bhoys'.

K Northover

units. The men who had volunteered being identified by the wearing of a khaki armlet bearing a red crown. Despite a large campaign the scheme did not succeed and conscription was now to be introduced. When Banbury and district recruiting for the 'Derby' scheme ceased on December 15 approximately 1500 men had attended the recruiting offices at Cow Fair. On January 5, 1916 Prime Minister Asquith introduced a Military Service Bill which made all single men between the ages 18 and 41 liable for conscription. Every man was to attest but those who had good reason could apply to Banbury Borough National Service Tribunal for exemption. From February 1916 this was held in Banbury at the Union offices and also the court room at the Town Hall. The Tribunal heard claims for exemption or postponement to later groups which much depended on the attitude of those hearing the case. They had to take due regard of the claims of industry and the hardship when refusing appeals in cases of financial, business or domestic difficulties. There had to be personal grounds for the appeal and not just being indispensable to an employer, the employer had to appeal and prove the case himself. Details and results of appeals were published regularly by the Banbury Guardian. If appealants were not satisfied with the results at the Banbury Tribunal the case could be heard by the Oxfordshire National Service Appeal Tribunal whose final decision was binding.

FROM THIS HOUSE
IS SERVING HIS

KING, HOME

AND

COUNTRY

A patriotic poster displayed in the window of the home of Pte Charles Benson, Oxford & Bucks LI in Queens Road.

K Northover

The first Military Service Bill proved to be inadequate and at the beginning of May a new Universal Conscription Bill became law, to include married men.

Those called were to report to the recruiting office in Bridge Street, but after January 1918 under national service organisation this was then situated in a room at the Conservative Club. The Royal Navy established a separate recruiting office in December 1917 at No 1 Horsefair, the Recruiting Officer was Petty Officer H Venus.

In March 1917 a demand for workers was made for men to volunteer to register for national service. The object was to form a register of the older skilled workforce in less essential trades and industries willing to replace men of military age in exempted jobs in the essential industries who could join the forces. The men were asked to sign a voluntary offer of service so they could be requested to undertake work of national importance if and when they were wanted. No volunteer would suffer any inconvenience or loss of pay.

Despite a huge advertising campaign, the National Service scheme was generally thought to have been a failure. The need for manpower continued in the forces and medical standards were lowered and the recruiters took a second look at those that had been rejected earlier. Women continued to take up work in the towns and factories. Locally many found employment at the filling factory but there was a great need for workers in the fields. In June 1918 a large recruiting rally was held in Banbury under the auspices of the Oxfordshire Womens War Agricultural Committee in connection with the need for an additional 30,000 women and girl volunteers for the Womens Land Army, to save the harvest for that year.

Robert Stevens (37), stationer, bookseller, and newsagent, 9, Horse Fair, asked for absolute exemption under the hardship clause, the business being the means of livelihood of himself, wife, and two children.— Appellant said it was a one-man business entirely, and, in answer to Dr Thorne, he said there was occasion for a medical certificate.— Appellant was exempted till 1st October, and recommended that he be examined by the Medical Board.

Josiah South (35), West Street, Grimsbury, clerk in the employ of Messrs. H. Stone and Son, cabinet makers, etc., asked for absolute exemption from military service of any description on conscientious grounds, and based his claim upon a humanitarian and moral point of view. He regarded all war as being an obsolute and barbarous method of settling international disputes, and was opposed to destroying human life under any circumstances. He also objected to what was known as non-combatant service, but would be willing to undertake clerical work if absolutely necessary as national service. Letters in support of the appeal were enclosed from Mr. W. C. Braithwaite, Mr. W. L. Whitehorn, Rev. A. D. Belden, Rev. J. Green, and Mr. A. Boulton.—Exempted from combatant service.

Messrs. Samuelson and Co., flour milling, agricultural, and general engineers, applied for absolute exemption for G. Robinson (34), of Cadoxton, Glamorganshire, an out worker on flour milling machinery, and millwright engaged in repairs and renewals of flour mills. He was a specialised and skilled man, indispensable, and engaged in a certified occupation.—Dr. Thorne objected on the grounds that the firm had had already too many exemptions.—Exempted refused.

Messrs. Samuelson and Co. also made application for the absolute exemption, on similar grounds, of E. H. May (38), of Gainsborough, also in their employ as an outworker on flour-milling machinery.—Conditional exemption till 1st September.

Application had been entered by the Town Clerk (Mr. A. Stockton) for the absolute exemption of G. H. Oakes (29), Bath Road, Borough Accountant, Accountant to the Education Authority, and Registrar of the Cemetery, as being included in the list of certified occupations and necessary for the keeping and control of the finances of the borough and education authorities.—Conditional exemption granted as long as he remained in his present occupation.

Banbury Advertiser

Report in the Banbury Advertiser of July 13, 1916 giving the findings of the Banbury Borough Tribunal held at the Courtroom, Town Hall on the previous day. The panel consisted of the Mayor, Alderman J Bloxham, T O Hankinson, Councillors W J Harding, W E Wood and J Perry, Mr T Barrett, Mr H R Webb (Clerk), Dr Thorne and Mr Waterhouse (Military Representative)

" Please Sir, our 'Erbert aint no need to worry about Conscription 'as he—? "

A comic postcard c1916. Oblique humour of concern that it would not be a 'short' war after all.

K Northover

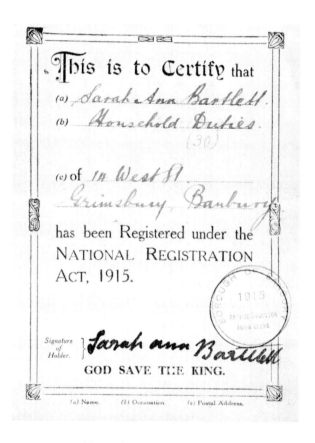

National Registration Card 1915.

Barry Davis

Certificate of Exemption belonging to Thomas Pargeter, a postman of East Street, Grimsbury
K Northover

Certificate of Registration for Alfred Lampitt. The Medical Officer comments on evidence of Valvular disease of the heart. Classified medical Grade C2.
K Northover

Name and address of new employer and date of employment when the holder changes his employment for other work of national importance.

TO BE FILLED IN BY RECRUITING OFFICIALS ONLY.

Date_____

Date_____

Date_____

8292 11871/701 10m (#) 6/18 J.P. Gp. 158
8417 19739/719 65m (6) 8/18

CERTIFICATE OF EXCEPTION

FROM THE

MILITARY SERVICE ACTS,

1916 to 1918.

This is not an exemption or protection certificate, but shows that the man to whom it is issued is entitled to be excepted from the Military Service Acts under para. 4 (b) of the First Schedule to the Military Service (No. 2) Act, 1918, conditionally on his being engaged in whole-time work of national importance.

In order that this certificate may be continued when the employment is changed to other work of national importance, the holder must return it to the office of issue with particulars of his new employer so that they may be inserted in the space provided and the certificate be recorded as continuing and returned to the holder.

Region
Regional Number *14 8957 .K.*   Certificate Number _____

THIS IS TO CERTIFY THAT
(full names) *PARGETER Thomas.*
of (Registered address in full) *47 East St. Grimsbury Banbury*

Occupation stated on National Registration Certificate *Postman*
now employed with (name and address of employer) *G.P. Office Banbury*

as a (present occupation) *Postman*
who left or was discharged from H.M. forces on (date) *9. 9. 17.*
is excepted from the provisions of the Military Service Acts, 1916 to 1918, if he continues to be engaged in whole-time work which is for the time being certified by the Director-General of National Service to be of National Importance.
Date *22 AUG 1918* 191 .   Signature *R. Turley*
for the Minister of National Service.

Written or stamped address }
of office of issue }_____ OXFORDSHIRE RECRUITING AREA
99, HIGH STREET, OXFORD.

The holder of this Certificate must sign it as soon as he receives it, and should carefully preserve it.
Signature of Holder *Thomas Pargeter*
R3/3762.

M. C. 2

Certificate of registration of a man who is willing to serve his King and Country as a Soldier for the War.

Name	Address	Date of Registration	Date of appearing for attestation	Age	Medical Officer's remarks
Lampitt, Alfred John	*1 Green Lane, Neithrop, Banbury*	*16 Dec, 1914*		*29*	

Station *Oxford*
Date *22 Dec. 1914*   Signature of Recruiting Officer _____ W. OWEN, CAPT., RECRUITING OFFICER, OXFORD.

Alfred Lampitt pictured with son Alf and daughter Clara mid 1915. Alfred Lampitt had volunteered on January 11, 1915 but was rejected for overseas service due to valvular disease of the heart. He was accepted into the No 5 Supernumeray Company National Reserve, 4th Oxford & Bucks LI. On October 20, 1915 he was posted to the 83rd Provisional Battalion. Dogged by ill health he was discharged as being no longer physically fit for war service on August 10, 1916 due to dilation of the heart. he continued to aid the war effort as an engineer at the Munitions Factory in Banbury.

K Northover

The band of the 17th Battalion, Rifle Brigade at Banbury in 1916, the band was formed mainly from professional musicians

Barry Davis

Soldiers Billeted in Banbury

During the war several regiments were stationed in the town and soldiers billeted in private houses. With the rise of food prices and hardship due to unemployment or personal circumstances the money received helped many families. Usually two or three men were allocated to a house, the only grounds for refusal being if there were no males in residence.

Troops were usually met at the railway station or boundary of the town and marched to their billets by men of the volunteers or boy scouts so that they would not lose their way. The first to arrive in Banbury were the 1st Battalion of the Essex Regiment who at the outbreak of the war had been stationed in Mauritius. They had returned home to England in December and detrained at the L&NWR railway station at Banbury on the afternoon of Monday, January18, 1915. The soldiers were greeted by a large crowd and flags were hung from business premises and private houses along the route to the town. This large column was taken through the town by the Territorial Band to the Horsefair where they were dispersed and led to their billets by scouts under the command of Scoutmaster Braggins, together with men of the local constabulary. Most of the men were billeted in the centre of the town as there were many houses in close proximity to the centre in those days.

A second train of troops arrived later and they were led by their own bugle band to Broad Street. The battalion consisted of 899 men and 25 officers and their headquarters were established at the Drill Hall, Crouch Street. Due to the foresight of the Mayor and various other local officials plans were at hand to

21

provide entertainment for the new arrivals. The Church House was turned into a YMCA style rest room. The Congregational Church, South Bar turned over its school room for recreational purposes as did the Adult School, the Baptist Church and the Marlborough Road Wesleyan Church which contributed its lecture room.

A fortnight later saw the arrival of nearly 1000 men of the 4th Battalion of the Worcestershire Regiment. This battalion had been stationed in Burma and arrived in England on February 1, 1915. After disembarking at Avonmouth they journeyed by Great Western Railway to Banbury. The first train arrived at 11.15 am on Tuesday February 2. On the platform the Mayor of Banbury Mr W J Harding welcomed the Regiment to the town. As soon as they had all left the train the men set off for the Grimsbury district of the town headed by the bugle band of the 1st Essex Regiment. A large crowd lined the route from the station and even school children were permitted to join in. The pupils of Christchurch (CofE) School, turned out to greet them 'little girls waving handkerchiefs and the boys cheering heartily'. The men were drawn up in West Street and taken to their billets by Boy Scouts. A second train arrived shortly afterwards bringing the total of troops up to 945 men and 23 officers. The regiment established their headquarters at the Wesleyan School in West Street. During their short stay in the town the regiments continued training in the countryside around Banbury and were generally very popular with the locals. Shooting matches, billiard tournaments, hockey and football matches were arranged against local groups such as the Britannia Works, the Early Closers and the newly formed Banbury Town Football Club. There were also very large turnouts for weekly services at the parish churches.

The two regiments and other units nearby were to be part of a new formation, the 88th Brigade, 29 Division. During the early months the Brigade began concentrating in Warwickshire and to much regret the 1st Essex moved to fresh billets in Warwick and the 4th Worcester's were to go to Leamington.

On Friday March 4, Banbury was astir early as at the homes where soldiers were quartered there were scenes of busy activity before eight o'clock when most of the leave takings were completed. It was a bright morning as thousands of townspeople said their goodbyes and cheered as the parade marched out of the town led by the Worcestershire's. Following behind by way of Parsons Street and North Bar at about 8.30 with drums and bugles the Essex's hove into view. As the piercing musical sounds moved away and began to fade they were superseded by the gentle procession of horses hooves drawing behind the field kitchens and ammunition wagons at the rear of the column.

By 9.10 am they had all left and a strange uncanny sense of emptiness descended upon the town.

Many romances and friendships were formed with the men during their short stay and when the Gallipoli operation began on April 25, and casualty lists appeared in the Banbury Guardian they had a special tragic significance for the people of Banbury.

K Northover

Band of the 19th Reserve Battalion, Kings Royal Rifle Corps, Banbury 1916. The band became famous locally for its high efficiency, and with its help many dances and concerts were arranged in the town for charitable causes.

As new units came into being during 1915 and 1916 Banbury once again became the host to thousands of fresh faced young men in uniform, the Kings Royal Rifle Corps and The Rifle Brigade. At a few minutes past noon on Monday January 10, 1916 a train entered Banbury station from St Pancras with 800 men of the 17th Battalion The Rifle Brigade. Once again but this time with more thoughtful looks the crowd cheered them by on their way to the Horsefair with their band leading them. They were dispersed from there to billets in Neithrop. The orderly room and depot was established at the Drill Hall, Crouch Street, followed by target practice at Crouch Hill Butts. Route marches in the countryside were arranged and field excercises were held in Berrymoor and other open spaces in the town. For recreation this time the men had the use of the Church House for reading and the Cadbury Memorial Hall by kind permission of the Grimsbury brotherhood. The battalion remained in Banbury until they were ordered to Wimbledon, becoming the 112th Training Reserve battalion.

At 10.30 on the morning of Friday, April 28 crowds gathered to wish them well as they left for the Great Western Railway station, the band led them away. Although no civilians were allowed onto the station before their train left at 11 o'clock some got round the restriction by buying tickets to Kings Sutton. In view of the fact that the population were now having to come to terms with the consequences of this war it is not difficult to imagine the emotional separations on the station platform.

On Friday, January 28, 1916 the 23rd Reserve Battalion of the Kings Royal Rifle Corps moved to Banbury from Andover in two trains arriving at 7.30 and 10.00 pm and was included in the 26th Reserve Infantry Brigade. The whole battalion of one thousand men were quartered in Grimsbury. A Sergeants mess was opened in an empty house and a battalion recreation room and canteen arranged.

On March 16 the 18th Battalion band was transferred to the battalion and gave several concerts locally. The band was dispersed on September 18 on army orders that all reserve bands must be discontinued and instruments returned. On April 14, 1916 the battalion moved to Wimbledon and became the 111th Training Reserve Battalion.

The 19th Reserve Battalion of the Kings Royal Rifle Corps moved to Banbury on February 1, 1916, the first Battle of the Somme being only five months away (July 1, 1916). Their headquarters were established at Calthorpe House, Dashwood Road. This unit became part of the newly formed 26th Reserve Infantry Brigade and occupied billets in the centre of the town. A change in the situation was observed with training being undertaken in the town and as soon as the men were considered fully trained they were drafted to battalions at the front almost weekly. Members of the 19th Battalion organised concerts and raised sufficient money to start a band which played for many charitable causes in Banbury. By May 18, this battalion moved on to Wimbledon also. According to the regimental history it was gratifying to note the appreciative

17th RIFLE BRIGADE and KING'S ROYAL RIFLES AT BANBURY.

"Fall in" is sounded; they parade;
The smart 17th Rifle Brigade;
And Banbury town in Oxfordshire,
Is our abode—we tarry here.

The King's Royal Rifles, fit and game,
Have earned an highly honoured name;
And here they're staying for a while
Before they tread a foreign soil.

In training for another day,
A bit to Kaiser Bill to pay;
And we shall do our level best
To send the foemen headlong "west."

We left our homes and kith and kin,
Anxious a victory to win;
The Huns will prove us "Tommies" real,
When our Brigade presents the steel.

"England expects" Lord Nelson said;
And if you have the paper read,
You know the men in khaki donned,
Is ever ready to respond.

At duty's call, our boys will fight,
To take a trench or storm a height;
And aid the Allies in the storm,
To drive Huns to a climate warm.

And when we leave the Banbury Cross,
The Lady on the famed "White Horse"
May, just for auld acquaintance sake,
Present us with a Banbury Cake.

PTE. W. WEST,
O.B.I.I

A poem by William West.

Barry Davis

send off for the 19th Battalion, greater than for any other unit. Crowds of towns people in far greater numbers than before and with greater voice moved the soldiers very deeply. They had struck a strong chord of friendship with the people of Banbury who would miss them. At Wimbledon the battalion became the 109th Training Reserve Battalion.

One other unit at Banbury during the period was the 22nd (Reserve) Battalion Kings Royal Rifle Corps they arrived in February 1916 and moved to Wimbledon in April becoming the 110th Training Reserve Battalion

Rfn Vernon Azariah (23744) 'F' Company
19th Kings Royal Rifle Corps poses for a
photograph at Blinkhorn's studio during the
regiment's stay in the town. Only 18 years old
he was a volunteer from Columbo, Ceylon
where his father was a native missionary. His
passage to England had cost him £100 of
which the Wesleyan College paid £50 and his
father the balance. It was unusual to find
someone coloured serving in a British
regiment at this time.

K Northover

The grave of Rifleman A Burgess 23rd KRRC in Banbury
Cemetery.

K Northover

There is a sad footnote to underline the state of mind of many of these young
men faced with this terrible war. Rifleman Arthur Burgess of 23rd Kings Royal
Rifle Corps suffering insomnia and of unsound mind, cut his throat at the
Bowling Green pub on February 29, 1916. Corporal Walter Reading of the same
battalion was found drowned in the canal lock by Kenches Mill on the Oxford
Canal on March 26. Their graves are amongst the Commonwealth War Graves
carved with the regimental badges in Southam Road cemetery.

Wounded troops stop off at Banbury station. Many of these pictured are Australians, survivors of the Gallipoli campaign, photo c late 1915.

OCC Photographic Archives

The Banbury Rest Station and Canteen

One of the first of Banbury's war activities to be started and the last to close was the rest station and canteen set up at the town's Great Western Railway station.

Its story began on September 10, 1914 during the period of the mobilizing of the British Expeditionary Force for France and Flanders. A letter appeared in the Banbury Guardian drawing attention to the fact that troops passing through Banbury station were so parched that they were drinking water from the station firebuckets. It happened that the letter was seen by a Miss Day, Quartermaster of one of the Red Cross detatchments who felt that as the nurses were only attending lectures at this time perhaps this was a bit of practical work that they could undertake. She consulted her uncle Mr Sydney Mawle Assistant County Director of the Red Cross Society for Oxfordshire who agreed to her proposal and together they interviewed Mr Short the GWR Stationmaster. He accepted the idea at once, promised every assistance and placed the General Waiting Room at their disposal. That same day sufficient nurses were found to form a detachment and by noon they were on duty at the station. Provisions had been secured and that afternoon two troop trains of 500 men had been served with lemonade. Within a few days friends in the town and district had recognised the work and gifts and offers of help were soon flooding in. This support continued without cessation up until closure.

The two Banbury detatchments of the Red Cross were organised into relays covering the period from 4 am until midnight, during the night periods they often received valuable help from men of the Red Cross and St John's Ambulance Brigade and from the Early Closer's Association* who also gave constant support in raising funds.

Gradually the waiting room was equipped, boilers and bread cutters were provided, huge thermos flasks kept a large supply of hot drinks ever ready, for as Autumn gave way to Winter coffee, tea and sandwiches replaced lemonade and fruit. With the number of troop trains taking men abroad and the ambulance trains moving northwards the War Office made Banbury an official rest station. It became Mr Mawle's responsibilty and a telegram was sent prior to trains departure from Southampton or Dover giving times of arrival and number of patients on board. The telegram usually reached here about an hour and a half before the train and this gave time for extra nurses to be found and supplies obtained and prepared so that by the time the train had arrived everything was in readiness. Tea, coffee, hot and cold milk were provided and each patient received a little cardboard tray containing a sandwich, bread, butter, cake, fruit and a chocolate and in addition a newspaper, cigarettes or tobacco and postcards on which to write home which were collected before the train left and were afterwards stamped and posted. The trains usually stayed here twenty minutes and had between 100 and 350 patients on board. The work was undertaken by the canteen staff as the station workers were called and the funding was provided by the British Red Cross Society but refreshments for troop trains had to be provided by means of fund raising and gifts.

In 1917 station helpers hours of duty were nine until twelve forty-five, twelve forty-five until four thirty and four thirty until eight of which they were expected to work at least two shifts per week. A list of those on duty was drawn up and published weekly in the Banbury Guardian. The uniform to be worn by the women helpers was a blue overall dress, sleeves, collar and cap and plain apron as per nurse pattern with black shoes and stockings.

Often after heavy fighting two or three ambulance trains were served in one day in addition to the normal flow of troop and ordinary trains. It was estimated that two hundred thousand men on Red Cross trains passed through the station staff's administrations. The work went on in all weathers, year in year out. During the summer the task seemed quite pleasant but it was a different story on dark stormy winter days and nights when the platforms were slushy, the roofs were dripping and a bitter cold wind would blow through the station. From early in the morning the staff were hard at work preparing for feeding

*This was a social club for shopkeepers on early closing day. They had a pavillion and sports field in West Street, Grimsbury which backed onto the railway lines

Wounded soldiers receiving refreshments at Banbury.

OCC Photographic Archives

Canteen staff at Banbury station.

OCC Photographic Archives

the troops and long after the town's inhabitants had retired for the night they remained at their posts waiting for the late trains.

The trains brought men from all parts of the British Isles and the Empire as well as from France, Belgium, Italy, Serbia, and America. In addition to troop and Ambulance trains the staff supplied refreshments to parties of convalescent soldiers, many Australians and Canadians often very ill or limbless who were being removed from base hospitals. These usually came back in batches of fifty and often at not more than one hour's notice. Also all soldiers and sailors travelling by ordinary trains were catered for. It is thought that some three million men were fed at the station during the war and the work was very much appreciated by the troops. There was a constant flow of letters from all over the world from officers and men coming from the trenches expressing gratitude. On one occasion 6,000 men were catered for in one day whilst an entire week saw 20,000 pass through.

When the Armistice was signed in November 1918 the staff were able to welcome and refresh the returning troops with tea, coffee and sandwiches. Above the platform was hung two stretchers with the words "Welcome home" and "Welcome back to Blighty" written upon them. Gradually the work lessened and it was decided to close the rest station on August 1, 1919. Five years of thousands of young faces, some never to return, dwindling away with that last train, its end light reducing to a tiny point in the darkness.

Miss Day must be given the largest amount of credit for the success of the project. She originated the effort and organised the work and was present day by day in all weathers. As Lady Superintendent she conducted the work with the Red Cross detatchments and when the Red Cross hospital was opened in Grimsbury she was appointed Quartermaster there. The work at the station continued with Miss Day retaining her position as Superintendent but with Mrs Arkell and Miss Whitehorn as assistants. Due to medical advice she resigned at the hospital and carried on her work at the canteen. Miss Canham became her assistant in 1916 when Mrs Arkell became ill, Miss Whitehorn became Quartermaster at the hospital.

In January 1919 Miss Day relinquished her position and Miss Canham and Miss T Bradford conducted the work until its closure. Alongside Miss Day must go a mention of Mr Sidney J Mawle, MBE whose unbounded energy and inexhaustible determination so largely contributed to the establishment of and maintenance of the canteen. Throughout the years Mr Mawle pleaded the cause and never failed to secure the necessary support. He was made Commandant of the Red Cross hospital and as treasurer managed the financial side of the work.

A business committee was formed presided over by Miss Day and consisted of Miss Canham (Secretary), Mr Mawle (Treasurer) with Miss Bradford and Mrs Metcalfe. The funds were raised by voluntary contributions from the civilian population as no soldier or sailor was allowed to contribute. Gifts of money and goods were received from the people of Banbury and neighbourhood.

Military personnel receiving refreshments from Nurses and helpers on Banbury railway station.
OCC Photographic Archives

Red Cross Canteen staff and railway station employees September 1916. Far left is station foreman, Mr Berry, far right Mr Lines, platform foreman and centre seated Mr S J Mawle.

K Northover

Miss Freda Day, seated centre, and Mr Sydney Mawle, Commandant, left of her, sit with a detatchment of VAD nurses.

OCC Photographic Archives

Concerts and other entertainments were arranged by friends, nurses and the Early Closers. Large sums of money were collected by the travelling public and collections were made on the platforms and trains by Mrs F Jones (who personally collected £700) Miss P Hood and other nurses.

Banbury canteen was the first to be provided by voluntary effort for the travelling serviceman and was in existence before the installation of the buffets at the London termini. When the King and Queen passed through the station on two occasions they noticed the work of the canteen staff and made enquiries concerning it. One Banbury Boy scout Mr Frank Miles who was helping with the refreshments had the honour of handing King George V a cup of tea and a Banbury Cake and shaking hands with him.

List of names of some of the canteen helpers

Mr S J Mawle	Mrs Barker	Miss Nelson	Miss Dawson
Dr Penrose	Mrs Wilkes	Miss Woolnough	Miss Stourton
Miss Bradford	Mrs Ross-Walker	Miss Jerrams	Mrs J Roberts
Miss Canham	Mrs King	Miss Cox	Mrs Cholmondeley
Mrs Metcalfe	Miss Jones	Mr & Mrs Jones	Mrs England
Miss Evans	Miss Claridge	Miss A Bennett	Miss Kite
Miss M Bradford	Miss E Claridge	Miss Godfrey	Miss G Trevor
Miss Robins	Miss Hayward	Miss Savage	Mr E Berry
Mrs Freemantle	Miss O Bennett	Miss M Tucker	Miss Underwood
Miss F Williams	Miss Whitehorn	Miss Gander	Miss Riddle
Miss Oakey	Miss Butler	Miss Sealey	Mrs Matthews
Miss Standege			

The Wesleyan Chapel, West Street, part of the schoolroom visible on the right.

Barry Davis

The Red Cross Hospital

Apart from the already established Horton General Hospital, local auxilliary hospitals were set up for the large numbers of wounded sent to the area. Several were in large houses outside town, these were suitable as they had large rooms for converting into wards and spacious grounds in which to set up huts or large marquees. A case in point was one at Farnborough Hall that had 36 beds for other ranks. It was affiliated to the 1st Southern General Hospital, Royal Army Medical Corps (Territorial Force) in Birmingham.

Mr Sidney Mawle Assistant County Director for the Red Cross in Oxfordshire had been asked in 1915 by the County Director, to open a hospital in Banbury. Permission was given by the trustees of the Wesleyan Chapel in West Street for the use of the schoolroom for such a purpose.

The Finance Committee consisting of Mr S Mawle, Mr Whitehorn, Mr Gillett and the Mayor Mr W J Bloxham undertook to provide thirty-six beds on October 15, 1915. This was duly carried out and on October 20 it was formally inspected by Lt Col G S A Ranking, RAMC Commanding 3rd Southern General Hospital, Oxford, to which unit the hospital was affiliated, and as everything was found to be correct was opened for use on Monday 25, 1915.

At 10.52 am a train arrived in Banbury from Oxford bringing the first

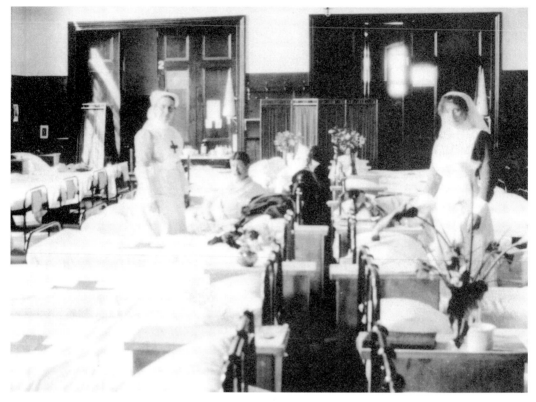

A view of the hospital ward.

OCC Photographic Archives

wounded. These were twenty-six men, of whom four or five were cot cases, the remainder being convalescent. The next day four more arrived bringing the total to thirty.

The hospital was staffed by a Matron, Miss Randall and trained nursing sisters aided by VAD nurses. Mr S J Mawle became Commandant with Doctors Beattie, Penrose and Prichard as Medical Officers. Miss Freda Day became Quartermaster with assistants Mrs L J Arkell and Miss Whitehorn. Nurse Harford took the position of Assistant Matron with Miss Beatties and Miss Harkin as Dispensers. The Rev G R Forde of Grimsbury was appointed as Hospital Chaplain.

The large schoolroom became the hospital ward with 36 beds arranged in four rows. At one end of this room, in an adjoining classroom, was the operating theatre and dispensary next to which were the lavatories and bathroom and a large geyser for heating water.

At the opposite end of the ward in the small schoolroom was the dining area and recreation room, furnished with furniture, pictures, rugs, and a piano by generous donations from the public. Between the dining room and entrance was the kitchen and pantries which contained two large gas cookers, a boiler and other catering facilities. Downstairs below these rooms were the stores and nurses personal quarters.

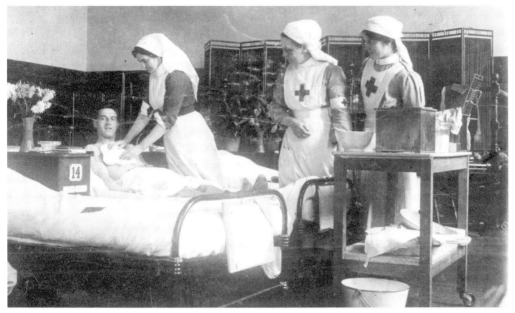

Nurses attend to a patient on the ward. Note the bed donor's name 'Stonehill' below the No 14.
OCC Photographic Archives

The main treatment of the wounded was carried out on the premises but as the need arose patients could be sent to the Horton Hospital for X-rays, specialist treatment and operations. The bulk of the general work was carried out by members of Number 4 detatchment and Number 30 detatchment of the Oxfordshire Red Cross Society (VAD). Some of the names of those noted were Number 4 detachment Miss F Ethel Jones, Miss Gladys Underwood, Miss Kate Canham and Miss D Chutter. Number 30 detachment Miss Monica Bradford, Miss F Day, Miss Helen Denchfield, Miss Alice Evans, Miss M Hill, Mrs Metcalf, Mrs Ross-Walker and Mrs H P Wilkes. Several members of these units served abroad and Miss Barford and Miss Fraser had both been under shell fire and bombing.

Patients could receive visitors during permitted periods and by November 4, 1915 these were as follows; Tuesday, Thursday and Saturday 2'o clock until 4. However a permit signed by Mr S Mawle had to be obtained first either from the Red Cross Office or from Mr Mawle's office at 22 High Street.

By October 1916 the hospital had 39 beds and the staff were a Matron Miss K Lyne with Assistant Matrons alternate weeks Miss Harford and Miss Owen, Quarter Master Miss Whitehorn, Dispenser alternate weeks Miss Beattie and Miss Harken with support from several auxiliary nurses.

Towards the end of 1916 plans had been made for a new open air ward. The Stroud family gave up the field rent free on which the ward, six marquees, Orthopaedic workshop, Recreation Room and Massage Room were built. The new ward was called 'Jersey' and was built by the building contractor of Banbury W J Bloxham. It was an open front hut ten feet long by twelve foot

wide seven foot at the front and nine feet high at the back. The front was boarded up to three feet high and waterproof curtains put up in pairs to each bay. It
was intended to place at least twenty-two beds in this ward bringing the total
in the hospital up to over sixty. Local residents, companies and organisations
donated beds. They were invited to name their bed, some examples were Mr
Stroud 'Mildmay' (after the family home), Bywater and Sons 'Britains Honour'
and 'Kitchener'. The new ward was officially opened on Wednesday,
November 22, 1916 by the Countess of Jersey who was President of the
Oxfordshire Red Cross Society.

As the hospital expanded hostels for nurses were sought in the town, one
being opened at 47 Middleton Road.

The patients at the hospital were well looked after by the staff and when-
ever possible entertainment was laid on for them. The wounded soldiers
dressed in their distinctive blue uniforms and red ties were taken into the
town, often in wicker bath chairs, to be entertained. The Conservative Club
and the Banbury Mechanics Institute allowed them free use of their premises.
Mrs J A Gillett provided the use of the recreation room at the Bluebird in Bridge
Street as did the Co-op at their Assembly Rooms in Broad Street. The patients
took part in Whist Drives, fun races (egg and spoon), three-legged races and all
kinds of sport including football, cricket and bowls. These were often played
against local teams and organisations, such as the Discharged Soldiers and
Sailors, Early Closers and Foresters. Charitable organisations often ran day
trips for the wounded and there was never any shortage of volunteers to take
them out for an evening's entertainment. The patients often held their own
concert parties and even had a musical group calling themselves the 'Beatties
Blue Boys Band', armed with whistles, cornets, fire tongs and other makeshift
instruments.

The local Red Cross Hospitals produced their own monthly paper called
the "Whizzbang" the first of which was printed in September 1916. It was for
patients past and present to inform them of developments in the hospitals,
changes of staff, numbers of patients and other relevant facts. Also it gave the
chance to publish soldiers jokes, poems and letters and give news of ex-
patients on their return to the front line. Often men returned to the war and
were killed. This was obviously very sad for the staff, but they also had their
share of heartache caused by the war. The Quartermaster, Miss Whitehorn, was
distressed when her brother Lance Corporal L Whitehorn 9th Royal Fusiliers
was posted missing on October 14, 1916. After frantic enquiries including those
made of troops and Red Cross trains passing through Banbury station, it was
eventually established in November that he was wounded and a prisoner at
No 1 Kriegsgefangenlager, Parchin, Germany.

In 1918 Mrs Kennedy the cook, who lived in Centre Street received news
that her son Frank had been accidentaly killed while serving with the
Grenadier Guards.

By the autumn of 1917 the hospital had 115 beds and staff consisted of the

Patients and one of the nurses pose in front of the Jersey Ward extension at the rear of the hospital. Note the New Zealand soldier centre of the back row.

OCC Photographic Archives

A view of inside the 'Jersey Ward'.

OCC Photographic Archives

Mr Sydney J Mawle, MBE Commandant of the
Red Cross Hospital.
K Northover

Dr N C Penrose c1930.
Banbury Advertiser

Matron Miss E Porter, sisters-in-charge, Miss Lee and Miss Gorman, Quartermaster Miss Hill then Miss Blencowe and Dispensers Mr Gorman and Miss Hudgel.

At the end of the war fifteen more beds had been added. The hospital was finally evacuated on Tuesday, May 13, 1919, the last party of patients leaving by the 9.57 am train. Some fifteen hundred cases had been treated at the hospital and only three patients had died. Two of these during the influenza epidemic late in 1918, early 1919.

An incomplete list of nurses shown at the time of closure:

Sister Eastwood, Sister Allen, Sister Deverall, Sister Randall, Sister Wormald (Quartermaster), Miss Bradford, Miss Ethel Jones, Miss Denchfield, Miss Cooper, Miss A Cooper, Miss W Cooper, Miss Hawtin, Miss Stroud, Miss Cox, Miss Dulak, Mrs Kennedy (Cook), Mrs Dean, Miss Whitenhall, Miss Marshall, Miss Collis, Miss Dunbar, Mrs Beattie, Miss Lickorish, Miss Claridge, Miss Trevor, Miss May Dommett, Miss Blencowe, Miss Massey, Miss Skinner, Miss Chuter, Miss Smith, Mrs Turney, Mrs F Jones, Miss Creed, Miss Page, Miss Giles, Miss Sealey, Miss Curtis, Miss Pulker, Miss Thame, Miss Sladen, Miss G Ward, Miss Evans, Mrs Barker, Miss Whitehorn, Miss Goddard, Miss Whinney, Miss Durran, Miss Lowe, Miss Hill, Miss Fowler and Miss Raikes with Mr C Warner and Boulter as Wardsmen.

With Compliments & thanks
To the Owner of this
Album. Sgt. Kacselau J.C.
14 B. R.B.

AUG. 18, 2ᴺ 1916

I WISH YOU HEALTH

I WISH YOU WEALTH

AND HAPPINESS IN STORE

I WISH YOU HEAVEN AFTER EARTH

WHAT CAN I WISH YOU MORE

Pᵀᴱ. A. TAYLOR .14 . 8ᵀᴴ ROYAL. FUSILIERS . RED CROSS. HOSPITAL. BANBURY

WOUNDED. AT. VERMELLES FRANCE. MARCH 18ᵀᴴ 1916

Pages from a nurse's autograph book signed by patients of the Red Cross Hospital

Banbury Museum

So far removed from the horrors of war, a Red Cross summer fete at Wykham Park in 1915. An impromptu moment for these wounded men to try to put out of their minds the effects of pain and suffering.

Barry Davis

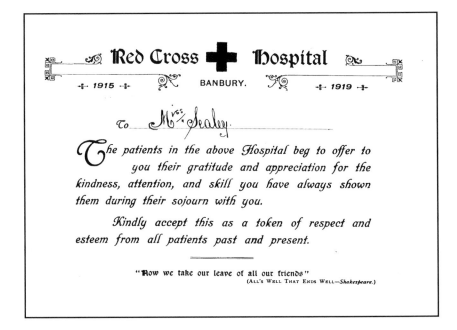

A vote of thanks from the former patients at the Red Cross Hospital for Nurse Sealy

Barry Davis

Two munitions workers in their factory overalls. The lady on the right is Isabel Taylor.

Mrs Audrey Tanner via Nancy Long

National Filling Factory No 9

As the war progressed it became apparent that the peacetime arrangements for the production of weapons and ammunition were going to be totally insufficient. Factories all over the country were busy manufacturing arms and munitions, but there was a shortage of suitable sites on which to establish the necessary filling factories. Many sites were investigated but most proved unsuitable either by the very nature of the ground or for the simple reason that there were no readily available rail or other transport facilities.

Packing ammunition boxes. When completed, barrows and trolleys, with rubber wheels, were loaded by the men and taken away.

Mrs Audrey Tanner via Nancy Long

Inside one of the filling houses. Shells were despatched to ordnance depots or direct to the channel ports for transport to the front.

Mr E Lester

However urgency was such that a number of sites up and down the country, hitherto considered to be unsuitable for any kind of industry were acquired for establishing of the filling factories. One such site was that just outside the town near the village of Overthorpe, by the 'Bowling Green' pub. This site was found in December 1915. The factory had originally been planned for Watford but the land there was subsequently rejected as unsuitable. The Banbury site was later extended and referred to as 'National Filling Factory No 9'. It appears to have originated in two stages. In 'A History of Banbury' by William Potts he records that two filling factories were erected, one at the foot of Overthorpe Hill and one adjoining the Corporation Farm. The initial Lyditte filling factory was built on an area of land comprising 142 acres adjoining the London & North Western Railway. By the end of 1917 a further 106 acres of land had been acquired on which a larger factory was erected. The whole of the site now comprised 248 acres with building area of 263,332 square feet, approximated capital expenditure of £150.000. It is recorded that in March 1917 a total of 993 men and 548 women were employed there. On March 31, 1918 the capital expenditure was recorded as being £173,973.

It appears that there was a proposal to carry on manufacturing munitions at Banbury after the war, due to the inevitable expansion of the site, as it is recorded that three NFF's were to be retained which were at Hereford, Perivale and Banbury.

During the 'breaking down' period after the war a total of 103 males and 72 females are recorded as being employed dismantling and disposing of grenades, bombs and shells. The proposal for the continued manufacture of war materials seems to have been short lived and the factory closed down around 1924.

National Filling Factory No 9 under the managing directorship of Mr H Bing commenced production in April 1916.

The factory buildings comprised of wooden structures on concrete foundations some of them surrounded by large earthworks strengthened with brickwork. These mounds and embankments were designed to prevent the spread of fire and contain the effects of any explosion should they occur.

The factory was connected to the L&NWR so that the loading and dispatching by rail was facilitated. There was a short length of siding alongside the single line mainline and both were connected to the factory via a siding which on entering the site split into two and fed a system of seven separate sidings spanned by a footbridge approx 125ft long. The standard gauge railway system within the factory site comprised in all some $3^1/_2$ miles of track. Two steam locomotives worked on this, a Hudswell-Clarke 0-6-0 ST named 'John' which was made in 1909 and is thought to have been put to work around 1916. The second engine was an 0-6-0 ST supplied to the Ministry of Munitions by the Avonside Engineering Co in 1917 numbered 1770 and named 'Lidban'. The fate of the former is unknown but 'Lidban' was sold to Brymbo Steel Co where it arrived on March 7, 1919, there it was renamed 'Arenig'.

Munition worker Gladys May Neal (nee Nash) photographed in 1917, aged 25 years.

Geoff Neal

Buildings and Production.

Artillery Shells were the main items produced filled with high explosive, shrapnel or mustard gas. Also mortar bombs and some types of sea mine. A certain amount of small arms ammunition was dealt with including cartridges which were made in several workshops.

On reaching the factory workers went to a dressing room where they stripped to their underwear and donned overalls. Their job determined the type of clothing worn. Girls operating tramway trolleys were attired in khaki tunics and trousers and wet weather clothing was available. In sections where certain powders and chemicals were used such as Lyddite, cordite and powdered TNT the girls would wear white trousers and tunics with mop caps to match. They were also issued with rubber gloves and often masks. The work would be unpleasant and the material handled often discoloured and irritated the skin, for this, soothing powders and lotions would be available. There was also a surgery where workers could report any infections whereupon his or her job could be changed. Apart from when using mustard gas, which caused blisters, the work was not unduly dangerous to health and any discolouration soon passed off. These premises were jokingly referred to as 'the yellow room' and the girls that worked in there were called 'Canaries' or 'Copper Queens'.

At lunch times or ending of their shifts the workers took off their overalls and caps in the changing rooms and stepped over the clean/dirty barrier and left the area. Working conditions in the filling sheds were reasonably comfortable the sheds being of necessity warm and dry. They were well lit and heated by steam, the temperature had to be carefully regulated as excessive extremes could affect the materials being used. An extremely clean environment had to be maintained at all times, the floors covered with linoleum were washed and scrubbed frequently. Women stood at long tables filling shells with Amatol from buckets. Amatol, (Ammonium Nitrate and Trinitrotluene also known as TNT) was melted by steam which was brought into the loading chambers by pipes from the boiler house. On the tables were boxes of transit plugs, wooden hammers and little cotton exploder bags already filled with powdered TNT, which were designed to amplify the impulse given by the fuse. As the workers filled each projectile with its high explosive Amatol they tucked in the exploder bags and screwed in its transit plug which would be replaced at the firing site by the proper nose fuse.

The filling houses were usually manned by four workers, two men and two women. Each shed was served by a pathway of duck boards for the workers and connected to other parts of the site by a 2 foot gauge tramway on which wooden trolleys were propelled by hand with the various types of ammunition from stage to stage of their manufacture. The shells arrived empty and lifeless and departed as powerful weapons of war. Small shells were filled and packed in boxes to be dispatched directly to the front, this was fascinating work and often messages were slipped in and answers and souvenirs were

Workhorse of the factory, the Hudswell Clarke 0-6-0 saddletank 'John'.

Barry Davis

Engineers staff No 9 National Filling Factory c1918. back row left to right Mick Wise, Jack Powell, Mr Gillett(?), Ralph Austin. Centre row (2nd) Joe Hitchcox, Alf Lampitt, Mr Butler.

K Northover

sent back in return. In the packing sheds boxes of ammunition were labelled and stencilled and moved along platforms with rollers to the main stores. There the boxes were stacked prior to being loaded on to the trains.

There were periods during 1916 and 1917 when extreme demands were placed on resources of the factory. In November 1916 Captain Snowball, the Works Manager, issued instructions for the calculation of the weight of acid (Picric acid also known as Lyditte) melted by each shift. On Friday November 17 the day shifts work was 630 cans melted with a total weight of 26, 840lbs. On February 1, 1917 thirteen trucks each containing sixty-three 9.2 inch shells were dispatched at 11.00 hours. On February 5, five trucks each containing two-hundred and twenty 6 inch shells, also twelve trucks loaded with 9.2 inch shells and fourteeen trucks containing five thousand 60lbs shells were dispatched at 15.00 hours.

During the three days 6, 7, 8 February 1917 a total of fifty trucks containing some twelve thousand shells of assorted calibre were dispatched, emphasising a period of very hard work, filling shells, inspecting and testing them in order to make sure that trucks could be loaded at such a rate. Records show that this activity continued for many weeks, all schedules being strictly adhered to and co-ordination with railways maintained to ensure that all deliveries to the armed forces were honoured.

The production allocation for the week ending March 3, 1917 was as follows, seven thousand 9.2 inch shells, ten thousand 60 pounders and fifteeen thousand 6 inch shells. The work was equally divided between two units, seven melting houses being required and employing twenty-two tanks. There was always one or two tanks kept in reserve in order to bring up the quality of the acid required so that there would be no difficulty experienced through bad gas etc, likewise there would be a filling house available should output fall. A despatch dated May 30, 1917 records that all shells used by British batteries on the Italian front came from Banbury No 9 Filling Factory. The quality of the ammunition was highly praised and factory employees were congratulated and ordered to continue their good work.

In August 1918 instructions were issued from the Royal Arsenal at Woolwich concerning 18lb shells charged with HE. Strict precautions were to be taken when filling the shells with liquid and any shell when inverted showing moisture leakage from the filling hole was to be rejected. All steel shells were bonded for 24 hours and iron ones for 48 hours with constant inspections taking place. Rejected shells were taken completely away from the filling area for disposal.

On December 9, 1918, after the Armistice had been signed, filling work was still being carried out. Personnel were surprised when the following notice was posted by Captain Snowball, 'I have received from headquarters the following report forwarded from France. It will be noticed that the attack referred to was made on September 30, 1918 and in connection with this I may say I promised the controller of gun and ammunition filling, on behalf of this factory, sixty thousand 18lb HE filled shells and twelve thousand 4.5inch HE by September 20. The last shell was completed and boxed by 9 pm on the evening of that day'.

The report continued;

'The new British mustard gas was used for the first time in the artillery preparation for the Fourth Army attack on the Hindenburg Line on September 30, 1918. This was one of the decisive battles of the end of the war, as the Hindenburg Line consisted of a series of strongly fortified positions which the Germans thought almost impregnable and its capture enabled a rapid advance to be made ending in Germany's collapse.

Two nights before the attack several villages near the line and many strong points and gun positions were shelled with mustard gas for six hours. In the latter case the effect of the gas was seen at once as the hostile batteries ceased fire and remained silent for twenty-four hours or longer. A captured artillery officer said that the gas was 'Sehr Schlim' (very bad).

The German infantry seems to have been surprised by the new gas; many of them did not wear gas masks and consequently suffered heavily. Prisoners from many regiments said that they had numerous gas casualties, amounting in one case to 25% of their total strength. Stretcher bearers and medical orderlies admitted that a number of gas cases had passed through their aid positions the morning after the bombardment. Ration parties were gassed and some of the enemy's troops were without food for twenty-four hours.

The attack was successful, the Hindenburg Line being pierced on a wide front, and there is no doubt that the casualties and disorganisation, caused by the mustard gas shelling helped materially to diminish the resistance offered by the enemy and to reduce our own losses.

It will be a great satisfaction to the munition workers engaged in making the gas to know that, thanks to their months of strenuous and dangerous work, we were able to use the new gas with such good effect in battle which had an immediate influence on winning the war.'

Safety and Discipline.

A tremendous amount of ammuniton was produced at the factory so it was important that the utmost precautions were observed at all times.

When on site workers had to wear rubber soled shoes, jewellery had to be removed including rings and wristwatches and no metal object was worn or carried. Foremen and women supervisors strictly enforced these regulations.

Matches and other smoking related materials were strictly forbidden in most parts of the factory. One workman Dennis Hickenbottom was found to have a small quantity of tobacco in his possession in a danger area. He was subsequently fined £3.

The layout of the factory was arranged with safety in mind. the actual loading chambers had strong walls but flimsy roofs, allowing, with the

A group of ladies at No 7 Filling House

Mrs B Healey

occurence of an explosion, for the blast to go upwards and not outwards. Large earthworks were formed to help localise any such explosion.

The risk of fire and explosion was fully recognised by all the workers and frequent fire drills were carried out. Mrs Doris Mold (nee Gaffee) remembered;

'We often had to attend fire drills. On one occasion the officer in charge asked "what we would do if one of the huts caught fire?" One of the girls replied, "We would be across those b*****ing fields as fast as the rest of them!"'.

Only one fatal accident occurred during the whole four years of the filling period and this was in the department known as the, Can Wash House, in 1917. However during the breaking down period, after the war, there were five fatal accidents.

Air raids were another great fear and instructions were issued to chief foremen as to the procedure in the event of an air raid warning. On the order 'take air raid action', all lights were to be extinguished, gas to be turned off, fires to be banked, shells containing explosive to be plugged, all doors and windows to be shut, any acid in the tanks to be left and all the staff and workers to retire from the vicinity of the factory. On the 'all clear' work as usual was to be resumed immediately.

In June 1917 Captain Snowball found it necessary to remind personnel that despite the importance of their job, munitions workers could be dismissed for ordinary breaches of factory rules and regulations, providing certain proce-dures were carried out. Despite the clampdown on drinking brought about by

A group of factory clerical staff, back row left to right, fourth, Isabel Taylor, tenth Mr Partridge.
Mrs Audrey Tanner via Nancy Long

the DORA regulations incidents still occured. One example resulted in a certain Augustus Kenny appearing in court in December 1917 charged with being drunk and assaulting a police sergeant at the site. Despite denying the charge, Kenny was found guilty and fined £1 on each charge.

In relative terms the munition workers were well paid and were often the subject of envy from workers in equally important but less publicised jobs. The factory was operated on a shift system and the average pay was 25 shillings and 9 pence (£1.29) per week daily rate and 30 shillings 3 pence (£1.51$^1/_2$) per week night rate. In addition a bonus was given for each shop upon the amount of work produced. Under the same scheme workers could gain from 3 shillings to 16 shillings (15p - 80p) per week extra. Trolley girls were given 6 pence (2$^1/_2$p) extra on day work and 9 pence (4p) on night work plus the average bonus of the shops they supplied. Girls working on the special powders were paid 2 shillings (10p) extra per week with an allocation of hot cocoa or milk twice per shift.

It was not all work however, by 1917 a recreation club was formed at the factory and a large billiards table with a charge of 6 pence per hour and a smaller table at 3 pence an hour was made available. Subscriptions to the Club were 1 penny a week. Facilities for tennis, cricket and football were also pro-vided. In the Spring of 1917 someone suggested that the girls in No 2 section at the factory should challenge the girls of No 1 section to a charitable football match with proceeds going to the Red Cross Hospital in West Street.

Concerts were held at the Recreation Club with vocal and instrumental music. In March the munition girls were themselves the subject of a charitable drive when subscriptions were asked to provide a hostel accommodation for the many workers who came from outside the Banbury area. Premises

National Filling Factory No 9 workers and members of the factory fire brigade c1916. Third row, seventh from right Lucy Walker(nee Holton).

Mr Walker

The Bowling Green pub on the Overthorpe Road. The entrance to the works was on the left side of the pub, where the lorry is in fact. Access for the staff was also found via the end of Merton Street.

Bill Simpson

Womens football was something of a novelty 85 years ago. However, in a good cause, munitions girls of No 1 section (above) met a team from No 2 section on a wet and windy day in the spring of 1917 at the Britannia Works ground. Both teams were dressed in regulation kit, the distinction being made by No 1 section wearing a blue tie and No 2 wearing a red. Lack of experience was no deterrent to the ladies and after an enjoyable game No 2 section emerged the victors by six goals to two. Lt Dicker, the fire officer of the factory acted as referee. The girls above unfortunately are only named by position which is goal keeper E Jarvis, full backs A Vickers and G Marshall; half backs C Hone, G Vickers, M Paulter; forwards M Booth, D Jarvis, A Hitchcox, A Lambourne and (holding ball) Captain M Garrett.

Mrs Audry Tanner via Nancy Long

The winning team No 2 Section, goal keeper M Fleetwood; backs N Laskey and D Buckland; half backs M Humphris, A Humphris and F Goodwin; forwards I Warren, M Rennie, M Allen, P Begram and A Cowles as centre forward and captain.

OCC Photographic Archive

previously occupied by the London City and Midland bank were secured as a hostel for women munitions workers and war workers.

There was always a friendly atmosphere and an aura of comradeship at the factory. For example, it was the practice of each shift to partly fill the shells ready for the next shift to complete them, this enabled continuous production. Judging from experiences related by former employees a strict sense of duty existed at No 9 Filling Factory together with a spirit of comradeship and efficiency with meticulous appreciation for detail.

A partial list of Staff and their positions held from 1916 - 1918

Mr H Bing, Managing Director
Captain H W Snowball, DCM, Acting Managing Director
Mr D Berridge, Works Manager
Mr A J Larkin-Smith, Secretary
Chief Foremen: Mr C F Freeborn, Mr A Cook, Mr C W Fortescue,
Mr H Lester, Mr W McGrath
Foremen: Mr G Allen, Mr E Woodford, Mr O Maycock
Assistant Foreman: Mr J P Charles
Womens Supervisors: Miss Baldwin, Miss Dingle
Lady Superintendent: Mrs White
Accountants: Mr S M Galloway, Mr B Stevenson
Cashier: Mr F J Wilks
Works Foreman's Office: Miss D Gibbs, Miss Bull
Canteen Office: Miss Churchill
General Office: Mr D Fowler
Time Keeper: Mr F Fleming
Chief Storekeeper: Mr H E Murray
Storekeeper: Mr W Neal
Engineers Department: Mr J E Haskins, Mr W Rhind, Mr Hislop
Engineman: Mr Bedlow
Fire Officers: Mr Burchall, Lt Dicker, Lt Hateley
Factory Police: Sergeant R F Langford, Pc F E Lawrence

Part of a connecting gallery and blast wall retaining embanked earth on the site in 1981. The site was used by the armed forces as a practice range during the Second World War and in 1976 a Royal Engineer's sweep produced hundreds of pieces of ordnance. However during the construction of the M40 Motorway work was suspended on several occasions due to the unearthing of shells, one initially believed to be mustard gas of World War One vintage.

Bill Simpson

Another view of the site in pre-motorway days.

Bill Simpson

Group of Oxfordshire Yeomanry outside their tent. From left, third Sgt Len Gardner, fifth Pte Charles Hyde (killed in action 1915) sixth Sgt Percy Harris. Photograph sent by Norman Sheasby, killed 1914.

K Northover

Territorials and Volunteers

Before the outbreak of the war important restructuring had been made in the organisation of the Army Reserve as a result of the Territorial and Reserve Forces Act 1907. The old volunteer units had been dissolved and in their place the Territorial Army was created. The volunteer cavalry units or Yeomanry were no longer to be a separate force and were amalgamated into the Territorial Army. The Militia became the Special Reserve, the local volunteer infantry battalion the 2nd Volunteer Battalion Oxfordshire Light Infantry became the 4th Battalion Oxfordshire & Buckinghamshire Light Infantry in 1908. As previously mentioned the Oxfordshire Yeomanry Cavalry or Queen's Own Oxfordshire Hussars became a part of the new system representing the mounted volunteers. In 1910 the National Reserve was formed which was a voluntary register of all ranks that could be available for duty in time of national emergency.

The Territorial Army or 'Saturday afternoon soldiers' as they were often known, was very popular with the local men and there was rarely a shortage of recruits. In both the infantry and cavalry units many of the men had given years of service and had even served as regulars and volunteers in the Boer War. The 4th Battalion Oxford and Bucks Light Infantry had found their original drill hall in Calthorpe Street but before the war they moved to the old British Schools building in Crouch Street which they shared with the

K Northover

Men of D (Banbury) Squadron Queens Own Oxfordshire Hussars wearing service dress at the outbreak of the war.

Banbury men of the 1st/4th Battalion Oxfordshire & Buckinghamsire Light Infantry at camp at Shrewton, Wilts, August 7, 1912.

K Northover

Oxfordshire Yeomanry. The Banbury company's were designated 'C' and 'G' until January 1915 when the Battalion then adopted the four company organisation and became 'C' company under the command of Captain E C Fortescue.

In peacetime the men spent their evenings and weekends in military training and parades, taking shooting practice at Crouch Hill and attending an annual camp. Prior to the war a Mr Denchfield hired out two of his fields on the Easington Estate to the volunteers for shooting. This was for a fee of one pound per annum.

The men of the Oxfordshire Yeomanry always considered themselves a 'a cut above the footsloggers'. Their ranks were filled mainly by the sons of landed gentry, farmers boys and tradesmen, most of whom could ride and shoot and brought with them their own horses. The Annual Camp was for fourteen days and took place under canvas in several private parks in the county. One of these was Blenheim Palace owned by the Duke of Marlborough who had for many years been connected with the regiment, his sons Winston and Jack Churchill having been officers with the Yeomanry at this time. These camps were grand affairs with manoeuvres and attacks, skill at arms competitions

Banbury Territorials on manoeuvres in the New Forest, August 1907. Photograph sent home by Bert Stanton of 22 Bath Road, Banbury.

K Northover

and all kinds of sports including tent pegging, sprint racing for men and officers and lemon slicing (the slashing of a suspended lemon with a sabre) whilst passing at speed. Before the war the Yeomanry consisted of four squadrons but the War Department demanded three so one squadron, the 'B' Woodstock was disbanded and its men distributed among the 'A' Squadron Oxford, 'C' Squadron Henley and 'D' Squadron Banbury. On the order to mobilise the Yeomen were to report with their horses to their respective headquarters. The Queen's Own Oxfordshire Hussars were to have the distinction of being the

Men of D Squadron Queens Own Oxfordshire Hussars at camp c1911 wearing full ceremonial dress.

K Northover

first territorial troops to embark for France and being the first mounted volunteer unit into action.

The 4th Battalion Oxford and Bucks Light Infantry went to camp at Marlow on August 2 for its annual training, only to be recalled to Oxford within twenty four hours on the day before war was declared. The next few days were fully occupied with sifting and enrolling of recruits who were then posted to company's billetted in several of the colleges.

When the territorial force came into being it was intended solely for home defence and officers and men engaged only for home service. It soon became evident that the Regular Army would be insufficient to carry on the war. Therefore territorials were sent abroad to release regular units from their foreign stations, (on August 4, the local regular battalions , the 1st Oxford & Bucks Light Infantry were in India and the 2nd Oxford & Bucks Light Infantry were in Aldershot). This took up only a small part of the force available and those remaining were divided into two battalions consisting of foreign servicemen (1st line battalion) and home servicemen and recruits, (2nd line battalion). As the war progressed the 2nd line battalion the 2nd/ 4th Battalion Oxford & Bucks Light Infantry became an overseas unit instead of just a feeder of the 1st line, the 1st/4th Battalion and a 3rd line or reserve battalion was formed to continue this task. In 1915 the Home Service men were then sent to form the 83rd Provisional Battalion.

The Yeomanry had one overseas battalion the 1st/1st Oxfordshire Yeomanry (QOOH) and a home service battalion, the 2nd/1st Oxfordshire Yeomanry which later became a cyclist unit. The 3rd/1st Battalion was affiliated to a reserve cavalry regiment.

Kitchener's New Army

In an attempt to boost enlistment in 1914 Lord Kitchener appealed for recruits to form battalions for a, so called, New Army. Thousands came forward and with few uniforms, equipment or arms the training began in earnest. Many Banbury men went into the service battalions of the local regiment, the Oxford & Bucks Light Infantry. Those formed during the first year of the war, the 5th, 6th, 7th, 8th and 9th were engaged in training during the Autumn of 1914 through to the spring of 1915. The 5th Battalion proceeded overseas in May 1915 as part of the first new army (K1) and the 6th Battalion of the second new army (K2) two months later. These were followed in September by the 7th and the 8th (pioneer) Battalions of the third new army (K3) the 9th Battalion acted as reserve for the other four Battalions and by 1916 became the 36th Training Reserve Battalion.

Volunteer Training Corps

The outbreak of the war saw the raising of the volunteer force which was formed for men compelled to stay at home, yet who wished to be trained to help defend their country if the need should arise. Those recruited consisted of

Officers and men of the Oxfordshire Yeomanry parade in South Bar Street prior to the outbreak of the war.
Barry Davis

The Queens Own Oxfordshire Hussars under canvas at Blenheim camp, Whit Monday May 27, 1912. Men of D (Banbury) Squadron preparing feed for their horses. The officer in the centre is Lt A Keith-Falconer.
K Northover

Men of the Banbury Territorials fire a volley in the Horsefair during celebrations to mark the Coronation of King George V in 1911.

K Northover

men either unfit, over or under age for active service or who were in important occupations. In August 1914 detachments of the Oxfordshire Volunteer Training Corps were formed. These units raised subscriptions and funds to cover the expense of equipment and rifles. The men, then, in red brassard bearing the Royal cipher GR until in February 1915 when a green/grey uniform was authorised and issued in the July*. In November of that year the eleven various detatchments formed into platoons and companys and became the 2nd Battalion Oxfordshire Volunteer Regiment. The Banbury detatchment became the No 5 and No 6 platoon of No 2 or 'B' (Banbury) Company, with their headquarters at 17 Market Place. At this time the county regiments badges and shoulder titles, at private expense, were adopted. In mid-1916 the volunteers were reorganised under the administration of the Territorial Force Association. All men were attested and took the oath. Authority was issued for the wearing of khaki uniforms and all equipment was provided at the expense of the state. The armband was retained but was now issued in khaki bearing a crown and letters GR in red and this was to be worn when not in uniform.

All men of seventeen or over could join and also those who had attested

*At this time the unit comprised of some 100 men who were then based and trained at Hunt, Edmunds large malthouse.

under the Derby scheme could join until they were called up. Men temporarily exempted by the local tribunal were also accepted, a condition of the exemption usually being that they joined the volunteers. The men could only be called up to the colours as third line troops if there was an invasion and they were able to resign if they so wished. By Army order of July 1918 the unit became the 2nd Volunteer Battalion, Oxford & Bucks Light Infantry.

One of the main reasons for forming the Corps had been to relieve the regular troops of home defence duties. The VTC were sent to guard lines of communication, railways, wireless stations and if required, fallen aircraft. By far the most frequently performed duty was at Banbury and Didcot Army Ordnance Depot railway stations clearing the congestion of war equipment at weekends. Another task was the assisting with the guarding of some two hundred German prisoners of war housed at the workhouse in Neithrop. Security was observed by one *Banbury Guardian* reader to be rather slack and several prisoners escaped. One absconded on January 29, 1918 whilst working on the ironstone railway line on a bridge across the Warwick Road, (afterwards known by the locals as the German bridge). He was thought to have boarded a baggage train. A further two escaped on Sunday evening May 5, who went by the name of Ernest Lopatz aged 23 described as 5ft 4inches with sallow complexion, brown eyes and hair being of stout build. The other Franz Writz aged 24, 5ft 4 inches also with brown eyes and hair and spoke English. Both were dressed in clothes that bore a prison patch. They were not at large very long and were recaptured at Daventry on the following Wednesday afternoon.

OXFORDSHIRE NATIONAL RESERVE.

Stationed at OXFORD, KIDLINGTON and DISTRICT, and SOUTHAMPTON.

Here's to the National Reserve,
Willing to King and country serve;
Yes! every man in khaki donned
Stepped forth to readily respond.

No shirkers in the ranks are found,
For one and all are duty bound
To guard the bridges and the line,
Demanding sharp the countersign.

With Captain Brakspear at the head
The Oxfordshire Reserve is led;
Lieutenant Fortescue is there,
The varied duties keen to share.

The sentry, with his watchful eye,
Will bar the foe from coming nigh;
An enemy shall shrink and reel,
Checked by a bullet or cold steel.

On service, in King George's name,
At duty's post, 'tis Tommy's aim,
His calling nobly to fulfil,
Responding to *reveille* shrill.

Comrades-in-arms and hand-in-hand,
The Vets. in unity shall stand,
With wit and tact and common sense
For righteous cause and home defence.

Shall we protect the public? yes!
The troop trains, too, as you may guess;
The red cross train shall ne'er be wrecked,
Whilst faithful sentries still protect.

The Chipping Norton Company,
Are guarding prisoners, near the sea;
The Germans will regret the day,
If they attempt to get away.

Sir Athelstane and Lady Baines
Give exercise for soldiers' brains;
A Reading Room is furnished free
For Tommy Atkins, you and me.

And if the Kaiser swims across,
He'll find John Bull will win the toss;
We'll crush him and his fiendish host—
Play the 'Dead March' and sound 'Last Post

lorth Newington,
  Banbury, Oxon.

                                                      Pte. W. WEST.

One of William West's poem cards celebrating the work of the National Reserve.

Barry Davis

Oxfordshire National Reserve at Oxford Roll of 'onner.

"Read" this carefully. The company is up to full strength, possessing a muscular commanding officer able to "Break spears." Our two officers, Lieutenants Fortescue and Aldridge, still reside here, though they are both "left tenants." "Quarter"-master-Sergt. George requires another three-quarters to make him full master of the situation. Long "May" the sergeant live. Owing to the floods, we have a "Full-brook." One private lives on "Ridge's" food, his main object being to "Phil-lips" with both "Hans"; he is ever ready to "Pick-ett" up, and is the "Picket" of the company. We belong to the Oxford and "Buckenham" L.I. "King" "Cole's" a merry old soul. The sergeant shouted, "Rix-on" fire!" In feathered pets, we have "Robbins," "Cox," and a "Starling," and there is a "Hawk-ins" side the Orderly Room. A word to the "Wise": Beware of the "Pickett." We can spend "Franks" in France. We'll all be merry at the Feast of "Stevens." "Watts" the "Hughes" of a "Sadler" in the infantry? If Sweetheart "May" will go her way, "How-ard" it is to "Turn er." Victory will be ours with a "Fre-win." Private Irving the "King" is serving; he acts on the military stage. One comrade says the Kaiser is a "Heath"-en, and he'll never get to "Lunnon" town.

Charlie Dowsett and Steedon Jack
Are still upon the Germans' track;
Quinton and Wilkins do their best—
I am, yours truly, Wilhelm West.

Another of West's poems cleverley using the names of men serving with the National Reserve in the rhyme.

Barry Davis

The volunteer force was suspended in November 1918 and was finally disbanded in September of the following year. Three hundred and sixty four volunteers had served in the ranks of the 5th and 6th Banbury Platoons.

Twenty-two years later they would become essential in that feature of home defence, as the nation faced the peril of invasion and subjugation in 1940.

Some Former Members of the Unit
Banbury Platoons
5 & 6

Adams, R J	Alcock, J J	Alexander, C W	Allen, L
Allen, W	Allin G H	Anker, F	Anson, A W
Austin, F J	Bain, W L	Baker, J W	Balfour, M D
Bannard, E F	Barrett, F J	Bonner, G E	Bowkett, R H
Bray, H	Brooker, C F	Bull, W J	Burrell, A S
Bustin, J	Busby, A E	Busby, H J	Carter F
Cole, N	Cooke, S B	Commin, J E	Copeman, B H
Cooke, H	Coates, H J	Chadburn, F	Chamberlain, R F
Charles, E G	Cherry, F G	Cherry, G C	Cherry C W
Chilton, H	Ching, H J	Claridge, A A	Cleaver, F W
Cleaver, H	Cloney, G	Clutterbuck, W	Cunningham, W
Crisp, G	Cross, E	Davis, H	Dumbleton, S
Dutriene, R	Evans J H	Evans, H W	Evins, F H
Ellmer H F	Essex, C V	Francis, F B	Francis, L
Freeman, P H	Freeman, W	Forrester, T	Frost, C J
Ford, F C	Ford, F	Fortnum, C	Foster, A J
Fowler, A	Gardner, R H	Garnett, R	George, A
Gibbs H H	Gibbs H W	Gibbs, W J	Giles, A E
Gilkes, P	Goodway, C C	Goodway, E J	Goodman R J
Grant, T	Grant, W	Green, E	Green J Rev
Green, R	Grigg, T A	Hale, C A	Hall, J E
Hall, F	Hamer, N A	Harris, F G	Harpert, T
Hartwell, C	Haves, R	Hazelwood, W	Headland, J
Heath, T	Hicks, J T	Hirons T A	Hobbs, W
Hobday, J	Hollis, C M	Holmes, W C	Sergt. Major Hone, J H
Hopkins, G	Howes, F B	Hudson, H P	Hunt, C R
Hunt, J	Huckerby, F E	Humphrey, F	Humphris, F S
Iley, F T	Iley, J E	Isaac, A E	Jackson, W T
Jarrett, A M	Jay, A E S	Johnstone, J L	Jones, P
Key, F T	Kilby, R V	Kilby, A F	Kirk, G H
Knight, G F	Knight, A E	Leach, J	Leach, H
Lewis, R	Lilley, J	Lines, E G	Luckett, T C
Luttman, W C	Malings, C	Mark, W	Mander, C
Matthews, A A	Maule, N W R	McKeevor, W P	Meadows, A E
Miles, A E H	Middleton, A	Mold, H	Mold, G
Morland, B R	Mumford, A H	Needle, C J	Neville, J
Oakley, L	Olds, A H	Orchard, W S	Osborne, A H
Osborne, R W	Owen, W J	Palmer, W T	Palmer, A E
Pargeter, W	Pellatt, F	Penrose, N C Dr	Pettipher, A
Pewsey, E	Phillips, A	Plumbe, C L	Prescott, P W H
Prentice, J H	Prudham, T	Powell, S F	Powell, H

Propert, G	Pulker, G	Rathbone, F E	Rathbone, W A
Rimmington, H	Ringwood, H	Roberts, J W	Roberts, F J
Rowlatt, J E	Rymell, C H	Rymell, W R	Sainsbury, W R
Salmon, H	Salter, G E	Saxby, W	Scroxton, G B
Seeley, E F	Sharman, W H	Shepherd, G J	Shott, E W H
Shilton, E	Shrimpton, T W	Shrimpton, W H	Skey, A N
South, F	South, W H	Smith, T E	Stanley, F E
Steedon, C	Steedon, J	Steedon, F J	Stevenson, H E
Strong, J	Stuchbury, W J	Symes, T	Taylor, H
Thorne, F	Thornitt, E A	Titley, W	Trinder, W E
Trolley, W W	Trolley, A W	Turney, F J	Tysoe J T
Upton, J	Varney, A	Vince, A	Vickers, G D
Vowles, W J	Wakelin, E	Wakelin, R E	Walford, B H
Wallace, J	Walker, B	Walton, J H	Walton, T W
Warren, M L	Waters, E	Webb, T	Welch, E
Wells, W F	Wilkins, A	Wilkins, H J	Williams, J G
Wills, W	Wilks, F J	Wilks, H P	White, N J
White, N	Wood, W E	Wyatt, W H	

Certificate of attendance given to Pte Alfred Lampitt 2nd Volunteer Battalion, Oxfordshire Light Infantry.

K Northover

2nd Volunteer Battalion
Oxford & Bucks Light Infantry 1917
HQ & Orderly Room 17 Market Place, Banbury

Officers and Senior NCO's
Hon Colonel His Grace The Duke of Marlborough
Count Adjutant Captain W Frank Cooper
County Commandant L Col A D Godley, OBE
Hon Commandant L Col J F Mason, MP HQ Staff

Ajutant Captain E A Ffoulks, Eriviat Hall, Denbigh, North Wales
AssAdjutant QM Lieut H A Butler, 58 Bath Road, Banbury
MO Lieut J A H Mogg (RAMC)V Woodstock, Oxon

Orderly Room Clerk J Smith (LateRA)
Armourer Sgt W P Webber, 11 Grosvenor Road, Banbury
Sgt Cook G H Liddiard, Glympton Park, Nr Woodstock

Officer Commanding Lt Col A Stockton T D The Green, Banbury
2nd in Command Major G E Underhill, JP 10 Northmoor Road, Oxford
M Gun Officer Lieut H M Gaskell, JP Kiddington Hall, Kiddington
Chaplain The Rev Canon A J Jones, MA, The Vicarage, Banbury

No 2 or B (Banbury) Company
Company Commander Capt W Potts, JP, 51 Parsons St., Banbury
Com 2nd in Comm Lieut E L Fisher, Cloverfield, Banbury
Comm Platoon Off Lieut R S Barnett
Company Sgt Maj F W Denton, 5 Fairview, Banbury
Q M Sgt Bernard Smith, 53 Middleton road, Banbury

No 5 (Banbury & District) Platoon
Lieut R S Barnett, The Holt, Middleton Cheney, Nr Banbury
Platoon Sgt A J Butler, 49 Bridge Street, Banbury
Ord Room Sgt A E Field, Bridge Bank, Banbury

NCO's
Sgt E A King, Banbury; L Sgt A T Kimberley, Banbury; Cpl H G Osborne, Banbury;
Cpl W Thompson, Banbury; L Cpl F H Tyson, Banbury; L Cpl C P Clarke, Banbury

Privates

E Chapman	T Jones	W E Denchfield	C J Doyley
F J Simmons	F W Bidie	J H Turner	W Gardner
E Tyrrell	H Shaw	W R Day	J C Marshall
H Stevens	F L Durran	J H Fox	S Grant
T Gaydon	W L Chatfield	F St G Butler	J W Page
J W Hickmott	A Price	F Du V Rainbow	H W Bleach
H Brain	G Thorne	J L Robbins	W J Sainsbury

District
Banbury, Broughton, Wykham, Bodicote, Grimsbury, Nethercote, Overthorpe, Warkworth, Middleton Cheney, Thenford, Chacombe.

No 6 Banbury & District
Lieut E L Fisher
Platoon Sgt. C J Smedley, 64 Fish Street, Banbury
O Room Sgt A E Field, Bridge Bank, Banbury

NCO's
Sgt J E Harrison, Banbury
L Sgt F T Ansell, Banbury
Cpl V G F Lewis
Cpl W R Stroud, Banbury
L Cpl J T Money, Banbury
L Cpl F Stroud

Privates

A Court	G Hirons	C F Easter	W Moffat	E B Gardner
J Fuke	J E Mascord	H Humphries	W F Jelfs	H Mellers
P W Woolams	W Mann	C M Joy	R B Usher	S Treadwell
J Higham	G H Harris	L Brailsford	T C Hewitt	F Selwyn
F Smith	J Tobin	J Hazelwood	W Dunmore	W E Gardner
G Gardner	T W Pargeter	J H Turner	A Hughes	J A Taplin
J H Angell	A Varney	J Ketch		

District
Neithrop, North Newington, Drayton, Hanwell, Wroxton, Shutford, Epwell, Balscote
Shenington, Hornton, Alkerton, Horley

Pte James Tobin, Oxfordshire Volunteers, of the Globe Yard, Banbury. In 1918, at the age of 43 and married he became liable again for military service. The local tribunal granted him two months exemption on domestic grounds as he had three children and a wife in a delicate state of health.

K Northover

Discharged on and after August 16, 1918

No 5 Platoon
Corporal Wray, A J Private Castle, A H

No 6 Platoon
Privates White H O, George W F, Townsend E, Bellingham E F, Allen, W E

Men of the
Banbury
Volunteer
Training Corps
manhandling
an artillery
limber
*The Times
History of the
War*

Men of the VTC unloading ballast at Banbury.

The Times History of the War

Mrs L Mold

Men of the Banbury National Reserve.

The Q. O. OXFORD HUSSARS are
"holding their own" at OXFORD

Postcard sent from a soldier of the 2nd/1st Battalion, QOOH at Oxford in early 1915. The writer comments, 'What do you think of our boys, they ought to know better. I tell them they will see their error some day!

A temporary pass granted to Pte Bernard Bartlett of 14 West Street, Banbury. A pre-war territorial he had gone to France on March 30, 1915. He was discharged as unfit for further service on September 23, 1916.

K Northover

Memorial plaque given by King George V to the next of kin of Charles Frederick Hirons, 4 Fish Street, (now George Street) Banbury. L/Cpl C F Hirons of the 1st/4th Oxford & Bucks LI (TF) was wounded in action on July 14, 1916 at Skyline Trench, Pozieres during the Battle of the Somme. He died of wounds two days later

K Northover

Casualties of War

'He whom this scroll commemorates was numbered among those who at the call of King and Country left all that was dear to them endured hardness, faced danger and finally passed out of the sight of man by the path of duty and self sacrifice, giving up their own lives that others might live in freedom. Let those that come after see to it that his name be not forgotten.'

So reads the commerative scroll given by the King to the grieving relatives of servicemen who died in the Great War. Of well over 2,000 men from Banbury who served 340 gave their lives, there were also hundreds of wounded and permanently disabled. Such a loss of so many young men was bound to have an impact on the town.

Telegrams or official letters informing relatives of the death, wounding or disappearance of loved ones became a regular and feared aspect of the civilian experience. Mrs Rose Pargeter (nee Bliss) recalled that on hearing rumour of her brother's death she and others of her family intercepted the telegram so they could break the news gently to their parents.

The reporting of details of casulaties in the local newspaper was diluted for public consumption. Personal experiences could not be censored, men had to live through them and if they survived live with the recurring nightmares of them. A local territorial writing home noted that Private Dick Humphries of Warwick Road 'was left in a trench with his leg off and part of his face shot away'. This kind of information never reached print. The usual anodyne for the relatives was 'death was instantaneous' or 'he suffered no pain', It is true to admit that their grief would not be lessened by knowing every detail of his death. Some of course were killed outright with a bullet in the heart or head or the sudden explosion of a shell. However the awful truth of a hideous and agonising death could not be avoided in a war where flesh and blood were pitted against the greatest amounts of explosive ever used in warfare. It was inevitable that reality would be softened as the war had become too hideous a scenario to relate.

The great sadness of loss was borne for many years by the families. Any visitor to the Kings Road home of Mrs Clara Lampitt, the sister of Privates Tom and George Gibbard, would be struck by one thing. There on the living room wall she would proudly yet tearfully show the several photographs and the framed medals and memorial plaques of her dead brothers, it was a virtual shrine to their memory.

The end of the war did not mean the end of suffering for many soldiers, a miserable conclusion to darken the jubilation of victory was the severe flu epidemic of 1919. Men weakened by wounds and shock were to arrive home only to be followed by death from illness. Gas poisoning, gangrene and suicide added to the toll. Sergeant J A Vince formerly of the Oxford & Bucks Light Infantry died of his wounds in July 1919 and Scots Guardsman William Woodhall of Broad Street succumbed sixteen months later.

Sergeant Harry Stroud of the Oxfordshire Yeomanry had had his leg amputated in 1918 when it had been badly done. The result was that he endured extreme pain for many years until he could stand it no more. Tragically he took his own life in April 1931 aged only 45 years.

Children living in Kings Road were somewhat wary of a neighbour, Bill Nutt. Bill had become a victim of shell shock and had been virtually struck dumb. He would clatter down the street in his old army boots and trench coat, almost dragged along by his large black dog with whom he walked for many miles. He could not stop walking, under his breath he continually muttered and cursed but he would often stop and talk with my grandfather, Alec Batts communicating with a series of grunts and nods.

Company Sergeant Major 'Jack' Coggins, DCM recalled how he still suffered nightmares about things he had experienced almost 75 years previously. These men, 'survivors' were the terrible legacy of that war long after that last shot had been fired.

War is of course the most extreme shared experience men could have and returning servicemen often felt something missing on their return to civilian

Extract from farewell letter by G.O.C., 20 Div. :—
" I always had a feeling that whatever task they were given to do, their grit and determination would carry them through with it."

Extract from farewell order by G.O.C., 60th Bde :—
" On this occasion I should like to place on record the deep regret felt by the whole Brigade at the loss of this fine battalion. It came to FRANCE with the 20th Div., and has served in the same Brigade and same Division for 3½ years.

" During this time it has always been marked out by its sense of duty, its steadfastness and its discipline. Its fighting powers have been proved in the most important engagements in the War."

6th (Service) Battalion
Oxfordshire & Buckinghamshire
Light Infantry

RE-UNION DINNER
BANBURY

August 25th, 1928

HISTORY

Sept., 1914.—Battalion formed.
Sept., 1914—*July*, 1915.—At home, CAMBERLEY, BISLEY, BLACKDOWN, GRAYSHOTT, LARK HILL
July 21, 1915.—Advanced party and transport, to FRANCE.
July 22, 1915.—Battalion crossed to BOULOGNE.
July, 1915—*Feb.*, 1916.—Trenches, LAVENTIE, FLEUR-BAIX.
Feb., 1916—*July*, 1916.—YPRES.
July, 1916—*July*, 1917.—SOMME.
Sept. 3, 1916.—Attack on GUILLEMONT.
     Casualties : 8 officers, 272 N.C.O.'s and men.
Oct. 7, 1916.—Attack on RAINBOW TRENCH.
     Casualties : 13 officers, 230 N.C.O.'s and men.
July—Sept., 1917.—YPRES.
Aug. 16, 1917.—LANGEMARCK.
     Casualties : 3 officers, 150 N.C.O.'s and men.
Sept. 20, 1917.—EAGLE TRENCH.
     Casualties : 13 officers, 196 N.C.O.'s and men.
Sept. 30—*Dec.*, 1917.—Somme.
Nov. 20, 1917.—Battle of Cambrai.
     Casualties : 5 officers, 20 N.C.O.'s and men.
Dec., 1917.—YPRES.
Feb. 8, 1918.—Battalion disbanded.

     Total killed : 24 officers, 491 N.C.O.'s and men.
     Taken prisoners : 6 N.C.O.'s and men.

On February 6th, 1918, there were serving with the Battalion 2 Officers and 159 N.C.O.'s and men who came out to FRANCE with it in 1915.

HONOURS.

Brigadier General E. D. WHITE, C.M.G.
Lt.-Col C. R. C. BOYLE, D.S.O. and bar.

Military Cross.
     2nd Lt. J. E. ZERON.

2nd Lt. F. B. MITCHELL.	Capt. R. H. BELL.
Lt. G. W. WOODFORD.	Lt. R. G. PLUCKROSE.
2nd Lt. G. V. ROWBOTHAM.	2nd Lt. T. N. C. HARRIS.
2nd Lt. H. MONEY.	2nd Lt. B. J. HENRY.

D.C.M.

Sgt. F. J. COOKE.	L./Cpl. T. COOMBES.
Sgt. F. C. STANTON.	Pte. E. PARKER.
Sgt. R. BETTS.	Pte. J. R. CROXALL.

Military Medal.

C.S.M. W. WOODCOCK.	Pte. J. ALLEN.
C.S.M. E. GEORGE.	Cpl. J. T. CHILTON.
C.S.M. J. EAST.	L./Cpl. E. EVANS.
Sgt. W. EDGINGTON.	Pte. P. VINCENT.
Sgt. C. FOX.	Pte. F. COX.
L./Cpl. H. W. SEAR.	Sgt. D. W. LISSITER.
Pte. V. KINCHIN.	L./Cpl. G. F. CHAPMAN.
Pte. J. ELKERTON.	Pte. A. DALEY.
Cpl. GARRATT.	Pte. J. L. RADWELL.
Pte. E. V. PORTER.	Cpl. E. PATIENT.
Sgt. A. T. JONES (1 bar).	Pte. H. SMITH.
L./Cpl. T. COLLETT.	Cpl. A. T. JONES.
Pte. T. CLARKE.	Pte. E. W. SPOONER.
Pte. W. HUDSON.	L./Cpl. F. ADAMS.
Pte. F. JAMES.	Pte. P. T. WALKER.
L./Cpl. E. RICHARDS.	Cpl. S. W. DUNKLEY.
Pte. G. NEWELL.	Pte. A. CLEMSON.
Pte. W. CHERRY	Pte. A. E. CHAMP.
Sgt. W. WISE.	Pte. W. GRIMSTER.
Pte. G. WHITE.	Cpl. J. WILLS.
Sgt. W. FRENCH.	Cpl. T. W. CAMBRAY.
Pte. A. KIMBLE.	Pte. T. WILKINS.
Sgt. HANNIS.	Pte. A. G. RAWLINS.

Souvenier programme of the 6th Battalion Oxford & Bucks LI Re-union dinner at Banbury 1928.

K Northover

life. The men had endured something no homebound civilian could possibly imagine, it forged a very special bond of comradeship between them. Annual reunions gave them a chance to meet again and talk in a bitter sweet way about the years of hardship, the bond between them all could never be broken.

The Queens Own Oxfordshire Hussars (Oxford Yeomanry) held their reunion once a year and continued until quite recently until those remaining were unable through age to attend. At their reunion pride of place was afforded to 'D' Squadron signboard which had stood outside their billets in France during the war.

Battalions of the other local regiment, the Oxford & Bucks Light Infantry also had an annual get together in the town. These events were well supported and gave the old comrades a chance to share a meal, a drink and reminisce.

The first opportunity for the old soldiers of Banbury to reunite occured on August 7, 1919 when the town publicly entertained eleven hundred men who left the borough to fight for King and Country. It was estimated that over 2000 men served, of these 1100 were present, some 330 had died and most of the remainder were still serving, either at home or abroad. The reception took the form of a dinner followed by a concert. The Mayor, Alderman W J Bloxham gave an admirable lead in the arrangements and a public appeal by him resulted in a generous response from the public who came forward with subscriptions to defray the cost of the dinner and entertainment.

The building in which the dinner could take place presented some difficulty as there was no hall in the town which could seat the number to be dealt with. Messrs Hunt, Edmunds offered the use of their malt house but here the guests would have had to be distributed on different floors. A large marquee was also suggested but the catering committeee fortunately found a large workshop 60 yards by 10 in the vacant Cherwell Works which answered requirements. The use of it was granted by the owners British Gold Plate Manufacturing Company and it was taken in hand by the Corporation staff and thoroughly cleaned, lime washed and the floor made good. Even this proved insufficient and an adjoining workshop was added. However the lists of guests increased and three long tables accommodating an extra two hundred had to be laid out in the yard. The whole site was decorated with flags and streamers and over the main gates a banner was stretched across bearing the words, "Welcome Back to Blighty".

Mr W W Trolley of High Street and Bridge Street carried out the catering most efficiently. The menu consisted of roast and boiled beef, roast and boiled mutton, roast legs of pork and boiled hams, vegetables, salads, mixed pastries and cheese with beer and mineral waters with a packet of cigarettes and tobacco for each guest. The beer was generously given by Hunt, Edmunds & Co, Messrs Hopcraft & Norris, Messrs Blencowe & Co, Messrs Lucas & Co and the Hook Norton Brewery Co.

The dinner began around 6.40 pm with the Mayor taking the Chair alongside Lt Col Stockton, Major E C Fortescue. Major P Pickford, DSO, MC, Captain

G L Samuelson, Captain M W Edmunds, Captain Booth, Lieutenants R Lidsey and H Askew, Rev A J Jones, Mr E Samuelson and others being joined later by Lt-Col Sir Rhys Williams, Bart, MP, DSO. The band of the Comrades of the Great War played during the dinner which passed off pleasantly. However owing to the hot weather the temperature in the building became oppressive and it was decided to have the speeches and music in the open air. The Mayor opened the proceedings with a toast for the health of the King and an appreciation of the Royal Family. Next came Lt-Col Sir Rhys Williams MP for Banbury who spoke of the sacrifice of fallen comrades which was received in respectful silence. There followed a presentation of decorations to three of the assembled company, Private F G Tyrell, 8th London Regiment awarded the Distinguished Conduct Medal; Private S H Grey, Oxford & Bucks Light Infantry, Meritorious Service Medal and Lance Corporal A P Prescott Oxford & Bucks Light Infantry, Military Medal.

The Mayor then spoke of the part played by Banbury's servicemen in the war. Mr J Jordan of the Banbury branch of the National Federation of Discharged Soldiers and Sailors and Mr R H Prescott Secretary of the Banbury branch of the Comrades of the Great War then replied with speeches*

The proceedings were concluded with the singing of 'Auld Lang Syne' and the National Anthem. The entertainment was provided by Mr F Webb at the piano, the Oxford Glee Party and Mr Duke of Oxford and Mr Lomas of Banbury.

*Early in 1918 branches were formed in the town of 'Comrades of the Great War' and the 'Discharged Soldiers and Sailors Federation'. These were amalgamated into the British Legion that became the Royal British Legion.

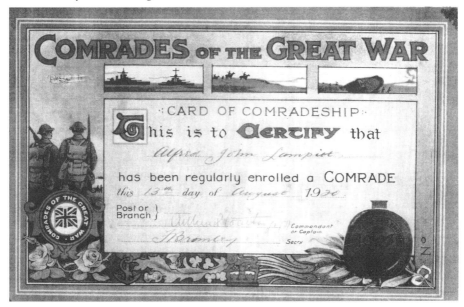

Comrades of the Great War membership certificate to Alfred Lampitt on August 1920.

K Northover

Ex servicemen of the Banbury Branch of the British Legion in the late 1920's. Back row Left to right; 3 Froggat, 4 Phil Bullock, 5 George Ellis, 8 Sid Stroud.
Middle row; 1 Blencowe, 4 Marsh, 9 George Stroud, 10 Harry Stroud, 11 Percy Heritage.
Front row 1 Percy Prescott, 2 Harold King, 3 Jack Wallace, 4 Fletcher, 5 R H Prescott, 6 F C Smith, 7 'Doc' Fortescue, 8 F J Wise, 9 R H Butler, 10 Bert Gibbs.

Mrs Woollams

British Legion Float c1930

Barry Davis

TO BE TAKEN BY THE ARMY
EVERY DAY !

All sides used humour to mitigate the true horrors that warfare had descended into.

K Northover

Gone for a soldier

After the initial shock of the declaration, war fever gripped the nation. The propaganda machine was in full swing with the national press and periodicals serving up grotesque or comic depictions of the 'beastly hun'. There was an initial rush to join the forces, due to the belief that, 'It would all be over by Christmas'.

Men joined for diverse reasons, 'to have a crack at the boche', with their pals, an adventure to break the monotony of their drab civilian lives. Some went out of moral obligation, some to escape from personal obligation and some just got swept along in the rush without really thinking about what they were going into. By mid 1915 there were almost a 1000 men from Banbury in uniform of some description.

At the close of 1914 the war had become a stalemate, with both sides digging in and trench warfare began. Massive casualties were sustained on both sides in attempts to break the deadlock and so many lives were lost to take an extra few yards of ground. This became evident in the local press where the 'war items' columns changed from tales of 'derring do' to sombre casualty lists.

By 1916 the numbers of recruits was falling dramatically. There was a reluctance to go as people began to realise that war was no 'picnic' no matter how it was dressed up.

Conscription was brought in and most went, with a willing resignation. Some, however, did not and were, mainly through religious reasons, unwilling to take up arms against their fellow men. Others had differing reasons for not wishing to go and these were heard through a local tribunal and widely reported in the *Banbury Guardian* and *Banbury Advertiser*. A few were prepared to take more drastic measures and there was one report in the local press in late 1916 of a Banbury conscript taking a noxious substance prior to his army medical examination to avoid being found fit for duty.

Once enrolled, the recruit would have a period of intensive and often brutal training before being sent off to the front. Their life became one of boredom and monotonous misery, intermingled with periods of pure terror. At home there was a constant thirst for news in those pre radio and television times. Of course the newspapers were heavily censored, so letters from the front were avidly read and the news passed around.

George Stroud writes to his girlfriend, Daisy Gibbard on December 1, 1914 having heard from his brother Sgt Harry Stroud QOOH and adds the latest pieces of gossip he has heard:'We had a letter from Harry yesterday, (Monday) and he says he is alright and in good health. They have had 79 hours in the trenches and they have returned for a rest. Jack Wasell is alright and in good health. They have received mother's parcel with two belts and two jerseys for Jack and Harry. He says it is very cold out there, the snow is about four inches deep.

Two young Litchfields on the bridge are in hospital with frostbitten feet. He said that chap of Ireland's has been shot but he said Jack is alright. So it only shows you what tales start in Banbury. There has been another man killed at Aynho by a troop train, in the same place where the other soldier was killed. It had got in Pott's window that England was expecting an invasion by the Germans. They were going to try to get in Yorkshire, it is reported that they have got 270,000 troops already loaded in vessels but don't expect they will get in England. There are train loads of soldiers going through Banbury for the coast, so there is something in that. A German Zeppelin dropped a bomb on a warship in Sheerness harbour. Will heard an engineer tell this to a woman on the train on Sunday on a journey to London'.

Rumours and gossip were rife. Alec Batts recalled hearing of the 'Angels of

Pte Frederick Fairfax (15349) 1st Battalion Coldstream Guards. Died of wounds France November 30, 1917. He was born in Banbury and lived at the Causeway. On April 5, 1915 he married Caroline Salter aged 25 of Warwick Road.

K Northover

Mons' when it was said a host of ghostly English bowmen appeared in the sky to terrify the Germans during the retreat. He was also told that trainloads of Russian soldiers had passed through Banbury station 'with snow still on their boots!'.

To add to the civilian frustration, soldiers on leave rarely spoke of their experiences and surprisingly many could not settle and were keen to get back to their comrades where they felt they belonged.

Once the men returned to the front their families settled down and could do no more than hope for their safe return. Often these hopes were cruelly dashed by the appearance, in their street, of the telegraph boy. People hoped against hope that he would not come to their door bearing bad news.

Much has been written about soldiers experiences of war and for the men from Banbury it was probably the same as the entire nation.

The following pages recount at first hand the actual experiences of three men. Two survived to live out their lives into age. The third remains a young man for evermore.

BUCKINGHAM PALACE.

I join with my grateful people
in sending you this memorial
of a brave life given for others
in the Great War.

George R.I.

A message of condolence from King George V that accompanied a memorial plaque.

K Northover

Cpl John Albert Benson 41st DAC Royal Field Artillery c1918.

K Northover

John Albert Benson

John Albert (Bert) Benson was born in Banbury, the son of Daniel G Benson, General Dealer and Sybilla of 6 Queen Street. Bert was a saddler by trade and at the age of twenty seven he enlisted in the Royal Field Artillery. He joined on September 28, 1915 and was sent to Aldershot for training with the Divisional Ammunition Column of the 41st Division a new formation created that month.

Training intensified during the next eight months and towards the end of April 1916 final preparations were being made for service in the field.

On April 26th the Division was inspected by H M the King who was accompanied by Field Marshall Lord French and General Sir A Hunter, Mayors of Boroughs and others who assisted in raising the various, mainly 'Kitchener' units were also present.

The Division received notice of mobilisation for France and entrained on

May Day 1916. Bert disembarked at La Havre with the Divisional Artillery on May 3rd and by the 8th the whole Division was concentrated between Hazebrouck and Bailleul. Bert's early actions were in the Somme area where his unit was engaged in the Battle of Flers-Courcelette in September and the Battle of Transloy Ridges in early October. By April 1917 he was serving in the Ypres salient in Belgium at the 41st Divisional Ammunition Dump at Ouderdom. It was here on April 15th that Corporal Benson performed a hero-ic deed that almost cost him his life for which he was awarded the Meritorious Service Medal. The citatation read as follows:

'Near Ouderdom, Belgium on April 15th, 1917 at the 41st Division Ammunition Dump the fuse of a faulty hand grenade under inspection began to burn. Seeing that an explosion was imminent and that there was no safe place to which he could hurl the grenade the NCO placed it between his legs. In so localising the explosion and saving his comrades he sustained severe injuries. Twelve or fifteen men were in the vicinity at the time of the explosion'.

So terrible were his injuries that there seemed little chance of him pulling through. He was taken to the No 17 Casualty Clearing Station at Remy Siding, Lijssenhoek where the orderlies were told to put him by the fire and keep him warm and comfortable. If he survived the night he would be examined in the morning.

The next day the Church of England chaplain at No 17 CCS sent the follow-ing letter to Corporal Benson's mother:

Dear Mrs Benson,

Your son Corporal J A Benson 44974 41st DAC came in here yesterday severely wounded in the abdomen by a bomb. He is doing well this morning and is cheery and bright. I think that you ought to know that he is seriously ill but I don't want you to give up hope or worry too much. He has the best of attention and everything will be done for him. We must leave the issue in God's hands. He wishes you not to worry about him.

Yours in great sympathy

D M Salmon

That day Corporal Benson underwent the major surgery that was to save his life. It is believed that the operation was the first of its kind and that the sur-geon later described it in an article, presumably in a medical journal or book.

On April 24th Mrs Benson received a letter from Bert's officer 2nd Lt. Jones:

Dear Madam,

I have refrained from writing about the accident to your son Corporal Benson until I learned further of his progress in hospital. I am glad to hear that he is progressing favourably and he seems to have passed the critical stage. I sincerely hope as I feel sure will be the case, that he will in time, completely recover from his wounds. From all accounts he appears to have acted most courageously, just before the bomb exploded and afterwards, he bore himself with the fortitude and pluck that always became him. I feel greatly his loss to me, his good natured way with the men, his energy in voluntarily helping them with their labours and the competency with which he carried out his duties made him not only popular but also a most valuable NCO.

While expressing to you my sympathies in the accident that has befallen your son, I can now express the confident hope that he may be spared to you for many years to come.

I am yours truly

O K Jones 2nd Lt. 41st DAC

It was while still at the CCS that Bert was informed of his award. His officer wrote to Mrs Benson on May 13.

Dear Madam,

Thank you for your kind reply.

I am glad to be able to inform you that your son has received as recognition for his act and services the Meritorious Service Medal which has been notified to the OC 41st DAC by the following telegram.

'The Field Marshall Commander-in-Chief has awarded the MSM to no 44974 Cpl J A Benson RFA. Please convey the Army Corps Divisional Commander's congratulations to the recipient'.

The Commander Royal Artillery adds his congratulations. Needless to say my congratulations and the men here are added. I have telephoned to his casualty clearing station and am informed that he has heard the news and it has made him ever so much better. They expect very shortly that he will be well enough to be sent to a hospital at the base.

Yours faithfully

O K Jones 2nd Lt.

The next day he also sent a note to Bert, still at the CCS.

Dear Cpl Benson,

My very best congratulations.

It was with great feeling of joy and satisfaction that we at the dump

A sullen German prisoner depicted on the 41st Divisional Christmas card for 1916. Sent with fondest love and best wishes from Bert.

K Northover

heard of your getting this decoration. Now we simply wish you a speedy recovery.

On ringing through to the CCS I heard that you were making rapid progress. I heard that you had left there otherwise I would have endeavoured to come over and see you, but we have been frightfully busy here since you left.

Well my best wishes.

O K Jones

In mid May the now Cpl Benson MSM was transferred to the base hospital. The Chaplain at the CCS wrote to Mrs Benson on May 16th.

Dear Mrs Benson,

Your son has just left us for the Base hospital, he is wonderfully fit and well and should be home very soon. I congratulate you on his winning the Meritorious Service Medal and I know he well deserved it. We are very sorry to lose him as he has been a great favourite here. He is a good fellow and has come through a trying time safely. I do not know anyone who has been nearer death than he has and lived. It was a fine piece of surgery that saved him and now he is practically himself again. We have all been glad to do anything we could for him and I think our prayers have been wonderfully answered.

Yours sincerely

D M Salmon CF 17th CCS

Whilst Bert was still at the base hospital his mother received a letter from one of her sons comrades.

24.5.1917

Dear Mrs Benson,

You will no doubt have thought that I am very lacking in courtesy since I have not acknowledged your very kind letter and gift till now, but I can only apologise and tell you that it has not been for want of thought but of time. We have been so very busy and it has been a matter of difficulty to even send a line to my wife.

However, many thanks for sending me the cigarettes and also the letter. I have not heard from Bert yet. It is probable that he does not feel very much like writing at present but our despatch rider went to see him a few days ago and said he seemed wonderfully bright. He was preparing for a journey to the Base. Personally I can only in very mild terms say of how glad I am that he is on the way to recovery and all those who knew him both on and off the dump are delighted with the honour bestowed upon him, for there is not the least doubt that by his own glorious self sacrifice he saved some of his friends from serious injury and perhaps death. When you write to him please tell him that I am anxiously waiting for a few lines from him.

With your own wish in your letter I can only join your wishes with my own and trust that at no very distant date our friendship can be renewed in the 'Homeland'. Bert's friendship to me is very dear and as I said in my first letter one that I hope will last.

Best of wishes to you and your family. Please tell them that I hope to see them, if as I often told Bert [censored]

With sincere wishes and hope for a happy reunion.

I remain,

Yours very sincerely,

J H Gask

By June Bert was back in England and had been sent to Nethercourt VAD Hospital (Voluntary Aid Detachment) at Ramsgate. Nethercourt's particularly appropriate motto was 'Never say Die' due to some wonderful recoveries made by cases virtually given up by doctors.

On June 6 he received a letter from his pal J H Gask.

Dear Benny,

Your very welcome letter reached me yesterday. I had been waiting patiently, knowing that you would write in your own good time and when you felt able to do so. Dear old chap the news that you are mending is the best of all, you cannot realise how much your presence is missed and the boys had inquired daily if I had heard from you. It is in my mind to address this letter with your decoration 'tacked on' congratulations, but we are not satisfied, it should have been the VC, you deserved it. But if you were handy you would give a telling off, 'I don't want thanks for a pally action'.

Write when you feel able to do so and as often as you like. I shall not forget my promise if you want me. Have heard from your mother and Benny I am longing to meet her, judging by her letters she is a mother to be proud of.

You would not know us here now. We have got 160 men working on the dump and today your old friend Mr Brewer has taken over the Infantry Ammunition. You will not be surprised to hear that I have put in for a Commission, of course it has not gone through yet but I am living in hopes. You are very lucky to get such a fine spot as Ramsgate and it must be glorious to have your mother and sister with you. Please remember me to them and tell

K Northover

Summerdown Camp, Eastbourne where Bert completed his convalescence.

them I am longing to meet them and most of all you.

I should have come over to the the CCS to have seen you but Mr Jones telephoned them one day and they told him you were going away. It was a great surprise when Wheatcroft found you there. Colonel Hurst had written to you but had his letter returned and seemed a little upset. He seemed to feel your loss.

Personally I hope that it will not be necessary for you to come out here again, but if it is, I hope you get sent to us again.

So old chap, buck up and get well and strong again for your 'wounding' was a sight that will live in my memory. I felt that I would have given anything to have saved you.

Best of luck and wishes old boy.

Hoping to see you in reality as I can in imagination, very soon.

Your sincere pal

J H Gask

Finally Bert was sent to Summerdown Camp, Eastbourne to complete his convalescence. He was medically downgraded and on December 31, 1917 was posted to the Labour Corps. Here he attained rank of sergeant and was finally discharged from the army on March 8, 1920. The remainder of his service being at home.

Little is known of Bert Benson and his life after the war. His great pal, James Gask never got his comission and remained as a sergeant. He too however survived the war. Bert became a solicitors clerk. He married Miss Florence Coleman of Newland Villas, Banbury on September 6, 1924 at St Mary's Church . They had no children, probably due to the extent of his war injuries. At some point they moved from the town and during the 1940's and 1950's were living at Salford, Hook Norton. After the death of his wife he was living back in Queens Road, Banbury where he saw out his days, living to a grand old age, he died in 1982.

Jack Coggins as a young bugler in 1914.

K Northover

William John Coggins

William 'Jack' Coggins was born in the village of Whichford in Warwickshire on January 18, 1896 and was christened at the village church. His father was a wood machinist and was working in Banbury at the time of Jack's birth. Just before he was twelve months old his parents moved to Banbury and resided in The Causeway. Here the remainder of the family was born, three boys and five girls.

He started school at the age of four at the Wesleyan School in West Street, Grimsbury and remained there to complete his education until he was fourteen years of age. At that age he commenced work as an errand boy for A E Field, a small drapers shop in Middleton Road. His wages were three shillings and six-pence ($17^1/_2$p) per week. His father was not satisfied with this and asked him to learn the wood working machinery with him at J F Booth & Sons builders in Butcher's Row, the site is now 'Hobson's Choice'.

At the age of fifteen he joined C Company of the 4th Territorial Battalion Oxford & Buckinghamshire Light Infantry as a bugle boy.

He had to attend two evening parades a week at the Drill Hall, Crouch Street and a fortnights camp annually. Part of his bugling duties was to sound the half hour dress for all parades, at Banbury Cross, the Town Hall and on the Railway Bridge. This army employment was of course part time and he was therefore able to continue working with his father.

So it remained until August 1914 when his unit were at their Annual Camp at Marlow the day before war was declared. They were immediately ordered back to the Regimental Depot at Cowley Barracks and their colours were deposited at Christchurch Cathedral, Oxford on the 6th of that month.

On August 25 they arrived at Writtle near Chelmsford, Essex. Here they spent seven months in training for the prospect of trench warfare that they were certain to encounter in France. Whilst at Writtle Jack was billeted with six other comrades with a Miss Small who at that time had a niece called Gwendoline staying there. During this time Jack and Gwen became good friends and after the war she became his wife.

The Battalion left Writtle on March 29, 1915 and marched to Chelmsford where they entrained for Folkestone. On arrival they embarked on the 'SS Onward' and crossed the Channel to Boulogne, France. It was nearly midnight by the time they reached their rest camp which was on a hill just outside the port. It was here on a frosty spring night that Jack had the experience of sleep-ing under a hedge.

After several days marching and resting they arrived at Ploegsteert Wood and here on April 8 went into the trenches for the first time to learn trench work under the instruction of the East Lancashire Regiment and the London Rifle Brigade. During this period Jack had his first experience of shell fire, machine gun and rifle bullets and the verey lights which lit up no man's land during the hours of darkness. It was here that the battalion suffered the first casualty on April 11. Private John White of East Street, Grimsbury was shot by a sniper. Some weeks after that the mortality of the situation was brought much closer when Jack lost a personal friend and neighbour from Banbury. Whilst peering out over a trench parapet Private Tom Sharman fell back shot through the head. Tom had died on the firestep with his eyes wide open in front of Jack and his other mates. A terrible moment to witness the reality of sudden death in war. Jack was eighteen years of age.

Around that time the Lewis gun was being introduced and Jack was detailed to attend the first instructors course using this new weapon. The course was held at Etaples and after passing Jack returned to the Battalion with promotion to Lance Corporal/ Lewis Gun Instructor.

The 'Oxfords' soon became experienced in trench warfare and between May 1915 and March 1916 they were busy instructing the 'green' young men of 'Kitchener's Army' as they arrived on the western front. Amongst them were the 5th Berkshires, 11th Royal Warwickshires, 8th Shropshire Light Infantry, 10th and 13th Royal Irish Rifles and the 13th York and Lancasters.

Between killing was the monotony of trench life, sniping, night patrols in no man's land, and never very far from your thoughts, the threat of attack. Jack

Lt Pickford (seated centre) and NCO's of C Company 1st/4th Oxford & Bucks LI. (Jack Coggins is directly behind his officer) in France c1916.

K Northover

recalled that on one night patrol they took a gramophone with them and set it playing records just outside the German wire. This prank incurred the wrath of the enemy, they opened fire and the patrol hastily retreated back to their lines. This is another example of how at the most desperate times men must resort to humour to keep their sanity.

July 1st was a date that remained in Jack's memory all his life. It was the first day of the 'big push' on the Somme. The scale of the slaughter, over 57,000 casualties on that one day alone, was not easily forgotten. His Battalion were at the time in reserve at Mailly Maillet. When it was apparent that the attack had failed they were sent back to Hebuterne and subsequently to Bouzincourt where they were given orders for an attack between Pozieres and Ovillers. On July 19 at 1.30 in the morning they went 'over the top' Jack was in charge of the Lewis gun section and in the first attack he arrived in the German trench carrying the Lewis gun loaded with only one magazine, his number two Dennis Taylor of Calthorpe Street who was carrying ten magazines was hit before he could reach the German line, as were others in his section.

The attack was held up for a time but after some very bloody and heavy fighting the objectives were achieved by the 23rd.

After that there was a lull when Jack and another man in his section were sent for a weeks rest behind the lines. They went to a casualty clearing station to assist in unloading ambulances bringing back dead and wounded, mostly dead. These had been in the front line trenches when the attack started. Jack found this business tougher than being in the front line. They worked nearly all night sewing up bodies in army blankets and preparing them for burial next morning. They then loaded them onto army G S Wagons, so many mothers' sons. They escorted the sad convoy to the burial grounds.

On arrival the bodies were unloaded and then laid side by side in a large communal grave which had been dug by French civilians. A burial service was read then it was back to meet the next batch of ambulances. That was their weeks rest.

During December 1916 the Battalion left this part of the Somme and by January 1917 were at La Maisonette opposite Peronne. Within a couple of months they were advancing after a retreating enemy. As Jack was leading his platoon towards Peronne they encountered a Uhlan patrol (Cavalry). Jack immediately opened fire with the Lewis gun killing several immediately including the officer in charge. After the carnage Jack retrieved a leather pickelhaube (spiked helmet) with its eagle badge on the front. This was sent back to Banbury where he was led to believe it was displayed in the Town Hall.

One evening whilst fighting in this area Coggins and his men searched for a place to rest overnight. They found a German dug out which was capable of holding a company of men 25 feet underground and was approached by a flight of twenty to thirty steps. Before taking the men down he went below to explore the place and found a dead German sitting on the bottom step. He kicked him down and found several other bodies on the floor which he cov-

Photograph picked up from a German dugout by Jack when on the Somme in 1916. The picture is addressed to Musketier Bruno Feustel, Infantry Regiment 82 and depicts his brother Ernst in a military hospital near Berlin on February 7, 1916

K Northover

K Northover

Centre, second row seated, CSM W J Coggins and men of C Company 1st/4th Oxford & Bucks LI in France in 1917.

Jack Coggins on a pilgrimage to the battlefields in the 1980's.

K Northover

ered with a number of German overcoats. It looked fairly quiet so he called his men down leaving two on sentry duty at the top. The rest were soon asleep on top of the bodies until someone eventually complained of the smell. It was then he divulged what they were lying on. Neverthless they still concluded that it was better than being outside so they continued to sleep. When daylight arrived they stirred and moved on leaving this mortuary to its silent depths.

When the regiment moved into Flanders where the summer offensive was to begin during August, Jack found himself at Ypres, he had been promoted to the rank of sergeant in No 9 platoon. During the first major attack on the 16th of that month he lost his platoon commander 2nd Lt H Jefferson so he had to take charge of the platoon himself. At this time a fellow Banburian, Captain Maurice Edmunds of Hunt, Edmunds Brewery was the company commander.

Photograph taken before 1st/4th Battalion moved to the front line in Italy in 1918. Left to right, rear row, second Italian guide, Sgt Peters, Edwards. Centre row Harmsworth, Coggins, Robbins.

K Northover

After the Ypres battles the Battalion was rested. It was during November that they heard they were to move with the 48th Division to Italy to assist the Italians to stem the Austrian advance. The journey from France to the battle-front took five days. The men were to find the mountains and the hill fighting very different from the trench warfare of France and Flanders. Things were very peaceful when they arrived and hardly a shell was fired. Before leaving France Jack had been promoted to the rank of Company Sergeant Major, he celebrated his twenty-first birthday in the Italian foothills.

After completing a period of training the Battalion spent some time on the Piave front before moving to Asiago Plateau at the end of April. On arrival the sector was fairly quiet but the British soon changed this. Artillery pounded the Austrian lines and patrols were undertaken.

On the night of May 14 Jack went out with a fighting platoon commanded by Lt H Miles, MC who had specifically asked for CSM Coggins. The object was to make a raid on an enemy outpost just outside their wire. It was a party of some thirty men who set out on that spring night with great stealth. Before long Lt Miles spotted some Austrian soldiers and took some pot shots. Jack shouted 'don't be a fool sir!', but the element of surprise was now lost. Several of their patrol were hit by a retreating enemy including Lt Miles who was severely wounded. Jack took command and led the men on, after first leaving two stretcher bearers behind to look after the wounded officer. The raid was successful as their instructions were to bring back one prisoner alive for identification (interrogation) purposes. The remainder were to be killed. Unfortunately the one Austrian prisoner met with an accident while coming through the British wire. The pin of a grenade in his pocket came loose and the bomb exploded killing him instantly and at the same time injuring one of Jack's men. For his part in this raid Jack was awarded the Distinguished Conduct Medal, his citation read as follows:

200100 CSM W J Coggins (Banbury) 3.10.1918.
'For conspicuous gallantry and devotion to duty when with a fighting patrol. When his officer became a casualty he took charge and led the platoon. He set a splendid example of pluck and initiative in the attack afterwards organised a rearguard which prevented the enemy, now reinforced, from interfering with the carrying in of a wounded officer'.

Night raids and patrols continued in an attempt to keep the enemy on their toes. On one particular occasion Jack recalled that he was offered a gold wrist watch by an Austrian who was badly wounded. He begged Jack to shoot him but before he could do so a shell exploded very close by and he had disappeared in the smoke and debris together with the watch.

On June 15 at 3.am a tremendous Austrian bombardment hit the British positions and at 7 am the enemy began to advance. The Battalion was holding the front line and the weight of enemy numbers began to overwhelm them.

Jack climbed up onto a road that ran through the trench to find out why the machine gun section wasn't firing. He was shot through the chest and stomach as he ran. Although practically choked with blood he crawled to the gun position but was shot again in the arm. He continued still only to find when he reached the gun position that all the gunners were dead and the gun smashed to pieces by the artillery bombardment. Some Austrians came upon him and taking him for dead cut off his DCM ribbon and two of his regimental tunic buttons, obviously for souvenirs, or identification of regiment purposes. Jack was finally picked up by stretcher bearers and taken to the first field dressing station, and then by an ambulance to a hospital in Genoa.

After six weeks there he was returned back to England to finish his convalescence. At this time he received a letter from his commanding officer in Italy who recommended him for a commission in the Infantry but all these were closed. The only commission available was in the Royal Air Force, this he took and joined three months before the end of the war. At the cessation of hostilities he had the option of staying in the RAF, which his financial position would not stand, or go back to the rank of Sergeant Major in the Oxford & Bucks Light Infantry. This he did and shortly after his marriage to Gwen Kersey at Eastbourne on April 3, 1919 was posted to the 2nd Battalion in Ireland.

He took up married quarters in Cork. During his time there he saw action against the IRA moving to trouble spots in Dublin, Tipperary and Limerick. He remained in the army to complete his 18 years service and then moved to Banbury to resume work at Booths. Having returned back to civilian life Jack's family grew, by now he had three boys and two girls. Just before the outbreak of the Second World War he took up employment at the Northern Aluminium Company on Southam Road.

On commencement of hostilities it was feared the factory may become a target for air attacks. The buildings were fully camouflaged and a dummy factory built some two miles away. The factory was protected by a battery of guns manned by regular soldiers and army reservists. Jack was asked by the works manager to join the army reserve and take charge of the gun site. This he did with the rank of Battery Sergeant Major. After the war he worked at the Alps Furniture Company, then Banbury Buildings, until the age of 70, finally working another ten years part time at Banbury College.

On many occasions Jack attended pilgrimages to France and Belgium continuing almost up until the time of his death. Jack died on January 31, 1994 at the age of 98.

Studio portrait taken in 1915.

K Northover

Gunner William Batts

Frederick William Batts was born on April 2, 1896 at West End, Chipping Norton, the eldest son of Frederick and Sarah Ann Batts (nee Young). Frederick senior was a shoemaker, as were his forefathers for many generations. During the year 1900 the family moved to Banbury and set up business in Broad Street and lived at $12^1/_2$ South Bar.

During the years preceding the Great War the family unit grew and 'Bill' now had two brothers Alec (b1901) and Harold (b1903) and also three sisters Florence (b1898), Dorothy (b1908) and Hilda (b1911). The family were devout Christians and young Bill became an active member of the Marlborough Road Wesleyan Sunday School and Church.

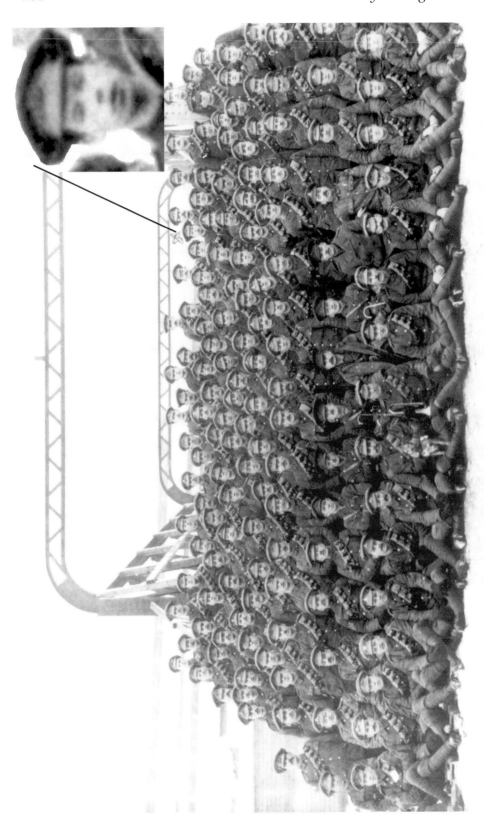

The 57th Siege Battery, Royal Garrison Artillery at Bristol in early 1916 prior to their departure for France. Bill Batts is at the back of the group, see inset.
K Northover

When war broke out Bill was employed with his father in the family shoe-making and repair business, although with his own shop, also in Broad Street. As soon as he was able he went to enlist. He had intended to join in a non-combative role, carrying on in his trade as a shoe repairer in the Army. However, the recruiting sergeant told him that fit young men with his constitution were needed in the Royal Artillery. On July 19, 1915 Bill officially became a member of the Royal Garrison Artillery.

He was first sent to Number 2 Depot RGA at Fort Rowner, Gosport, Hampshire for basic training. He was issued with his uniform and became Gunner 56891. In this role he writes to his parents.

Dear Dad & Mother,

Just a few lines to let you know that we have got our uniform. Our kit consists of the following articles; two suits, two pairs of boots, one pair of pants, one cardigan jacket, three pair socks, two towels, razor, shaving brush, brush & comb, soap, greatcoat, cap, toothbrush, puttees, two bellybands, blacking and canvas suit.
This morning we went before the captain and he read the Army Act to us.
The cap badges are only $^1/2$d each but they have not got any here now. We have a half day on Saturdays. I forgot to mention that we now have a knife, fork and spoon.

Last night I went in the coffee bar and while I was in there a fellow came up and told us he was pleased to see us and he is going to show us over the flying ground. He joined last December.

When you write to me put on the envelope No 5 room. We have some different beds now about the height of a cot. The boots some of the chaps have got are old ones, been repaired, but mine are now good ones.

We are going down to Gosport tonight again to see the Battleships. I hope you are all well as it leaves me the same. I don't know whether we shall get any pay but we are going up to see.
Will write again soon,
With best love to all,
from your ever loving son,

Will xxxxxxxxxxxxxxxxxx

From his letters he appears to have settled down quite happily into military life but still often thought of his family and home.

Dear Dad and Mother,

Just a few lines hoping that they will find you in the best of health as it leaves me in the same. I have just had a nice bath.

Gunner William Batts pictured with sister Dorothy in 1915.

K Northover

This morning I went to chapel, it is about a mile and a half from the fort. There was only seven of us, most of the chaps are C of E. Its a nice little chapel, a local preacher took the service.

I expect I shall send my clothes home tomorrow. If you do not get them by Thursday perhaps you would let one of them run down to the station and see if they are there. We went to the pictures last night. I am sending these cigarette cards for Harold, some of them are silk. In the top coat you will find a mouth organ for Harold and a cap badge for one of you in the waist coat pocket.

The aeroplanes are up in the morning about 5 o' clock. Some of the recruits have been served out with old boots that have been repaired. The quality of the repairs 'would not suit the Warwicks'. I have seen five aeroplanes up at one time since I have been here.

You might give Mrs Woodhull my address if you see her, I will write to her soon. I hope Alec and Harold are doing all they can to help.

There are some good fish in the moat here. We have a Yankee in our room don't half make you laugh. We shall not be able to get any pay before Friday. Its very warm here today, but its lovely and cool in these rooms.

With best love to all,

from your ever loving son

Will xxxxxxxxxxxxxxxxxxx

After training Bill was posted to his unit, the 57th Siege Battery, Royal Garrison Artillery which had been formed at Lydd in Kent on September 7, 1915. The armament of the unit at this time was to consist of 8 inch Howitzer guns. Training continued until February 1, 1916 when orders were received to mobilise at Heytesbury, Wiltshire for service in France. At 8.30 am the Battery began to proceed to Bristol. the unit strength at this time was six officers, and one hundred and fifty-four other ranks.

On February 2, 641 Company, Motor Transport Army Service Corps consisting of three officers and one hundred and eighteen other ranks, five caterpillar tractors and twenty-five lorries joined them at Woolwich for duty.

By February 3 the unit was at White City, Bristol and had taken over four 8 inch Mk V BL Howitzers. On the 28th the guns and transport left for Avonmouth for shipment. On March 2 at 2.10 am the personnel left by train for Folkestone and on arrival embarked on the 'Princess Victoria' for France. After disembarking at Boulogne the Battery marched to St Martin Camp in heavy snow and here they remained. After a brief stay the unit moved off to the fighting line. On March 8, they were at Lacres, on the 9th at Hesdin, on the 10 at Frevent, on the 11 at Talmas on the 13 at Walroy and finally they reached Martinsart near Aveluy Wood which was in the Somme sector.Here they took over from the 25th Siege Battery. They remained until July 20, and were heavily involved in supporting the infantry and in the preliminary bombardment which heralded the opening of the battle of the Somme beginning on July 1.

During this time the family heard very little from Bill apart from occasional field postcards saying he was well. In mid June 1916 his father received a letter from a chaplain at Lydd to whom the Batts' had obviously written a letter of appreciation of their good work.

Lydd

Dear Mr Batts,

We are proud to know your boy and the Battery to which he belonged, I have the name of twenty-five of them before me as I write. It was very kind of you to write and express your appreciation of our efforts. It comes to us as a great encouragement to hear now and then of good being accomplished. We have an earnest band of workers praying regularly for these men and we do hope that your prayers and others may be answered.

Again, thanking you,

Yours truly,

G A Vernon, (Chaplain)

From July 21th to 24th the Battery were at Beaucourt and from July 25th until September 27th they remained at Fricourt and Peace Woods. It was here during August that Bill was slightly wounded by the effects of gas and shell shock. It is very possible that British gas could have been the culprit as Royal Engineer Gas Units were in close vicinity at the time and the poisoned clouds were prone to floating in the wrong direction if the winds changed.

On August 5 Bill wrote home.

5-8-1916

My Dear Father and Mother,

Just a few lines hoping they find you all in the best of health. I am at rest camp for a few days, I had a touch of gas and also a bit of shell-shock but I expect I shall be back at the Battery in a few days.

Many thanks for the parcels received in good condition, I wouldn't send any more for a while, just a few cigs. I will say when I should like another. I have written to Vic, I expect she thought I had a nice cheek when you told her what I said, still I am looking forward to her return letter. We are having some exceptionally fine weather now. Thank Dorothy for her letter, I will write soon. I thought it would be alright with Flo and Charlie again.

There is no more news so will close,

with best love to all

from you loving son

Will xxxxxxxxxxxxxxxxxxx

The 'Flo' and "Charlie' mentioned in the letter were his sister, Florence and her fiance Charlie Pearson. Sadly Charlie was to die in 1918 before they could be married. He cut his hand whilst opening a corned beef tin, the wound turned septic and he died in hospital. His best friend Corporal Harry Lippet contacted Flo to add his condolences, they became friends and eventually married in 1920.

From September the Battery were at Contalmaison Villa, still in the Somme area, and here they would stay for the remainder of 1916. During quiet periods life became boring for the gunners and this was reflected in Bill's letters.

15.11.1916

My Dear Father and Mother,

Just a few lines in answer to your letter of the 5th inst. I hope you are all in the best of health as I am pleased to say this leaves me so at present. I expect before this you will have received my letters acknowledging the two parcels. It was quite a treat to have a nice drop of cocoa once more, it reminded me of the old times. In your last letter you mentioned about my short letters, the truth of the matter is that I cannot find much to put in them. I will try and write longer ones in future. I had a letter from Aunt Emily this week she says that she has sent a nice box of good things so I am looking forward to it coming any day now. I wouldn't send any more parcels for a few weeks unless I send, you could put the money by for when I come home on leave so as to have a good bust-up for once.

The weather is very mild for November.

Don't forget to send a few cigs. There is no more news so I will close now.

With best love to all.

Will xxxxxxxxxxxxxxxx

2.1.1917

My Dear Father and Mother,

Just a few lines to let you know that I am still quite well, hoping that you at home are in the best of health. I had a very good time down on rest. When we are on rest there is always plenty of food but when we are at the Battery there is hardly enough that is what I can't understand. I have had both parcels safely, one was on the road eighteen days but it was in good condition. I have also received Aunty Flo's parcel, that was nineteen days coming. She sent a fine pair of gloves and a nice muffler. We also had a parcel from the officers and friends of the Battery so I have done very well this Christmas.

As regards that shirt that you say you have at home for me, I think that it would be best to send it out as I don't see any prospects of leave just yet. Three of our fellows have been but it has been cancelled since, still it might come by now, I am longing for the time for when I shall be back at the old bench. Just now I hear that they have snow in some parts of England.

There is no more now so I will close,

With best love to all,

from your loving son,

Will xxxxxxxxxxxx

Photograph of the Batts family taken c1930. Left to right standing Dorothy, Sarah Ann (mother), Alec, Harold. Seated Frederick (Father), Nellie and Florence. Distant but unrelieved is a look of sadness in the eyes of Mr and Mrs Batts, which must have been repeated in all the bereaved parents in the town.

K Northover

On January 23th, 1917 the Battery were on the move once more. They were to move from the Somme area towards Arras in preparation for the battles that were soon to take place. On the 24th, they arrived at Saulty and remained for a week before moving on to Anzin. Here they stayed from February 1st, until March 10th finally arriving at St Catherine's on the next day.

Bill wrote home on March 10th.

10.3.1917

My Dear Father and Mother,

Just a few lines to let you know that I am still quite well, hoping to hear you at home are all in the best of health.
I received on the 7th your two letters dated 18th and 25th and I have also received two *Advertisers* . There does not seem to be much news in it lately. I expect you have my letter by now acknowledging the receipt of your parcel. We also have had a hard winter, first we had snow then about six weeks extremely hard frost then for a few days this month we had beautiful sunny weather, now it is again snowing hard.

I forgot to wish Flo many happy returns but she knows I never meant to forget her. I am glad to hear that you have plenty of work, but I am sorry that you have lost George for he must have been a great help. Still, I am glad Alec and Harold have made up their minds to do their best and I am sure they will never repent it. I only wish I was with you to give Dad and yourself a hand. It must be very hard for you both but if I am spared to come home again I will see to it that you don't have   such a hard time again. As you say Banbury must be very desolate place now all the fellows are being called up. In a few weeks time I shall be twenty-one. I remember a letter I had from Grandpa Young just after I came out here saying he hoped I should celebrate it in dear old 'blighty'. I thought that I should be able to at the time but I hope that I shall be home ere another year rolls by.

I am afraid all hopes of leave have vanished for this winter, I had hopes a few months ago when the Sergeant-Major told us one night on parade that it was starting in a few days but it was cancelled a few days later. I did not say anything at the time because I did not want to raise your hopes and then not turn up. Still I think they intend ending the war this year if they possibly can. It looks as if the Germans are hard pressed by their retiring and I see by the papers that the Turks have had a severe set back.

Would you mind sending to me a small writing pad, only a small one as they are more convenient for carrying about, and I could do with a pair of socks.

Please let me have Sid's and Charlie's address, I have lost them. I hope Dorothy is better, I will address my next letter to her as I think it is about time

I sent her one for her very loving letters and her presents. I often picture her and Nellie and the fine time we had together. Tell Nellie I want to know if she gave Frank Humphrey one of her curls when he went to join up.

I received your letter telling me about Gramp and Grans golden wedding too late but I will write tomorrow. Yes it was very sad about Elsie Haynes death, they seem to be unfortunate and I feel sorry for poor Aunt Aggie. I will try and let you have a line a bit oftener but don't worry if sometimes I leave it a bit long for I shall   be alright. I am sorry Holland has served you so shabbily, I didn't think he was one of that sort.

I think that this is the longest letter you have had from me since I have been out here, but it is a job to find anything to write about sometimes.

I see they have got over £1,000,000,000 for the War Loan, I believe it was more   than they expected wasn't it?

I don't think there is any more news now so will close.

Well fondest love to all,

from your loving son,

Will xxxxxxxxxxxxx

PS Please excuse scribble as my hands are cold.

Sadly this was to be his last letter home.

On the evening of March 30, 1917 Bill went to a neighbouring Battery, the 124th Siege Battery to visit some local lads there. It was to be the last time they saw him. The next day Bill was working at the munitions dump a few miles from his Battery. The German artillery began to shell the area and Bill and two of his companions, Gunners Pat Doyle and Tom Hewitt ran for cover into a small dug out. A shell landed directly on top of it closing the door and setting it on fire. The men were trapped, none survived. Bill had been two days from his 21st birthday. The next day the men were buried in the little Military Cemetery at Maroueil, nearby.

Back in Banbury letters of condolence flooded into the Batts' home. One of the first was from Bill's grandfather, William Young in London.

'Your telegram reached us about 12.20 today and the shock it was is beyond words to express. What your feelings are we utterly fail to realise'.

First hand information came from the front in a letter dated April 4. The Reverend Wilfred A Ferris, Chaplain to the Forces wrote.

'I feel I must write to you a few words of sympathy because your son was killed last Saturday, but I am sure you will be helped by knowing that he laid down his life for his country nobly and that he had a service at his funeral on Saturday. If you would care to write to the Director of Graves Registry and Enquiries you might be able to learn the position of your son's grave. I am afraid I cannot tell you in a letter, and his Battery (Siege) RGA could tell you

No. *Aw0/125/2347.*
(If replying, please
quote above No.)

ARMY FORM B. 104—82.

R.G.A. Record Office,
Dover
20th April 1917

Madam,

It is my painful duty to inform you that a report has been received
from the War Office notifying the death of

(No.) *S-6891* (Rank) *Gunner*

(Name) *Wm Batts,*

(Regiment) *57 Siege Bty, R.G.A,*

which occurred *with the British Exp. Force France*

on the *30th March 1917*

The report is to the effect that he *was*

Killed in Action

By His Majesty's command I am to forward the enclosed
message of sympathy from Their Gracious Majesties the King and Queen.
I am at the same time to express the regret of the Army Council at the
soldier's death in his Country's service.

I am to add that any information that may be received as to the
soldier's burial will be communicated to you in due course. A separate
leaflet dealing more fully with this subject is enclosed.

I am,

Sir

Your obedient Servant,

Officer in charge of Records. R.G.A.

18307. Wt. 15148/M 1365. 175M. 2/17. R. & L., Ltd.

P.T.O.

One of the most feared aspects of the war for the civilians was the receipt of a buff coloured envelope from
the War Office. This usually contained notice of a loved one being wounded, missing or in this case the
serviceman's death. A reminder that every loss at the front meant devastation for many at home.

K Northover

Gunner Albert Coleman 57th SB RGA of Castle Street West, Banbury who wrote to Mr Batts following Bill's death.

Louise Liboratos

An embroidered silk postcard sent by Bill to his mother.

K Northover

some more information. I am sorry for you but our God will help and comfort you wont he?

PS The Battery is of course very busy in these hard days.

On the same day a letter was sent by one of the gunners whom Bill had visited the evening before his death.

4.4.1917

Dear Mr and Mrs Batts,

I dare say you will be very much surprised to hear from me but I think you remember me. My name is 66651 Gunner G Powell, 124 Siege Battery, BEF and I used to work in the furnishing department of the CO-OP in Banbury as I have served you a good many times and I dare say by now you have received the sad news of the death of your son. I thought that I must write and tell you we spent a happy time only the night before he was killed outright at once.

It seems so hard to lose a comrade after having just found him out but he died a soldiers death. It happened about a mile from our Battery and I am going down first chance I get and you can rest assured that me and my chums will do our best to look after his grave while we are around this part. It is one of the ironies of fate and I hope the almighty will give you both strength to bear this very sad news.

Believe me to be your sincere friend.

Gunner G Powell

My home address is 25 Crouch Street, Banbury

Gunner A T Morgan of the 57th SB had written to his mother Mrs Ell of Wigginton on April 2nd, 1917 saying, 'I am sorry to say we lost W Batts on the night of 31st and two more of the old hands, so we are getting down the roll. It leaves about fifty now and we miss him as he was liked by all of the section. He had done his bit and was doing it then. I don't know whether to write to his people or not as I know they will be very much upset, him being the eldest. It will be a good job when it is over. There's something doing this time and if we don't finish it this time we never shall. Its surprising what they can stick.'

Obituaries appeared in the *Banbury Guardian* and *Banbury Advertiser*, references were made to his death at Marlborough Road Wesleyan Chapel and Sunday School where Bill had been a member of Miss Fairfax's young men's class. The family, continued with letters of support and sympathy.

Grandfather, William Young wrote on the 14th of April.

'It was a grief for us to see by yours (letter) that Harold was so terribly cut up, but we remember with affection and pride he always spoke of "our Bill" that one cannot wonder for he was a brother to be proud of. To Alec also our hearts go out and for his bravery in bearing up for your sakes we are thankful. We know how acutely he also feels the loss of such a brother and from our knowledge of him and his temperament I think his sorrow would be borne in secret. I am somewhat anxious to know has Flo heard from CP (Charles Pearson) lately, has he been informed of this sad happening? I feel sure to him it will be a sore blow. For in his affection to Flo, I think Will was equal to the affection of a brother. I sincerely hope he will be spared to return to you'.

On April 20, official notice of Bill's death was received from the Royal Garrison Artillery records Office in Dover. Three days later the family received a letter which appears to be in reply to a request by Mr Batts for further information regarding his son's death. It came from Gunner Albert Coleman, 57th Siege Battery, he was from 4 Castle Street West, Banbury.

23.4.1917

France

Dear Sir,

In reply to your letter which I did receive today the 23 inst. I will tell you all I know about your sons death, of course I do not know everything because I was two or three miles away from the spot where it occurred.

Willie was at work at a Dump and Germans did start shelling this Dump and they did all clear away from it and three fellows, your son and two more did go in a dug out and before they could get out a shell did drop on top of it, closing the door and setting fire to it, so none of them did suffer at all, death was instant. The three of them was buried next day, I did try to get to the funeral, but it was no use, they would not let me go. The name of the place where he is buried I cannot tell you in this letter but if I manage to get back to England I will tell you. I was going to write to you before but Corporal Walton said he would write because he did belong to his detachment and then Gunner Morgan said he would write so I said I would not write because I know you would not like to be bothered a lot.

Willie was very well liked in the Battery and all the following sympathise with you. I do not think I can tell you anything else on paper but if I was talking to you yourself I could explain a lot better.

Believe me to remain your friend.

Gunner A Coleman

same address if you wish to write back.

Whether Gunner Coleman relayed the full story of Bill's death in person to Mr Batts is unknown. Family tradition has it that Bill was given the chance of promotion to the rank of Bombardier but declined, thinking it would slow up his return home on demobilisation. If he had accepted may be he would not have been at the Dump on that fateful day. Just another irony of war.

On May 16 a letter was received from the Director of Graves Registrations and Enquiries at the War Office stating that Gunner F W Batts was buried at Maroeuil British Cemetery, three and a half miles north west of Arras.

The final official communications received by the family related to money owing to Bill by the army. On August 28, 1917 the War Office authorised the issue of eight shillings and five pence from Army funds to the estate of Gunner W Batts and finally on October 24, 1919 the sum of seven pounds ten shillings was received on account of war gratuity.

After the war Mr and Mrs Batts were issued with Bill's two war medals, the silver British War Medal and the Victory Medal, both inscribed on the rims with his number, rank, name and unit. From the King came a scroll of Commemoration and a Memorial Plaque bearing his name stating that 'he died for freedom and honour'.

The Batts family continued to live in Banbury. Flo moved away from the town after marrying Harold Lippet and had two children. Alec married his girlfriend Alice Goldsmith and they eventually moved into her brother's house in Kings Road where they stayed for the remainder of their lives, they had two children. Harold married and eventually settled in Gibbs Road with his wife and daughter. Dorothy never married, living mostly in Banbury until she died in 1999. Sister Hilda married Ernest Wilson and left Banbury, having two sons. Alec and Harold remained in the family shoe repair business, continuing in their trade in Parsons Street until retirement in 1974.

William Batts' grave in Maroeuil British Cemetery, three and a half miles north west of Arras.

K Northover

Members of the Stroud family in colourful costumes which were worn whilst collecting for the Red Cross Hospital, Grimsbury. Left to right Mary Stroud, Evelyn Stroud, Daisy Stroud, (nee Gibbard), Harry Stroud Jnr and Flossie Stroud (nee Webb).

K Northover

Fund Raising and Salvage

Besides the demand for men to join the forces there was also the demand for money. Flag days were a regular occurance for the usual funds such as the Red Cross, Belgian, Russian and French Relief and also local hospitals.

The number of funds became so prolific that towards the end of 1916 the War Charities Act came into force. This made it unlawful to appeal for money or articles for any war charity or raise money for the same by holding Bazaars, sales, entertainments or exhibitions unless the charity was registered and approved by the local Registration Authority. Those given such approval had to keep proper accounts together with minutes of all committee meetings and audited accounts had to be submitted to the Registration Authority regularly. Among local groups were the Banbury War Work Guild who amongst other good works sent a constant stream of knitted comforts and gifts to the soldiers and prisoners of war. In 1914 a local Territorial comments; 'the ladies of Banbury have also kindly sent one pair of thick woollen socks for each member of 'C' and 'G' Companies'. The Vicar of Banbury also received a letter of thanks from the Navy League for socks and helmets received from Banbury. In August 1917 they held a Country Fair in People's Park which raised £900. In April 1917 another group, The Mesopotamian Comforts Fund held a Banbury

Saint George's Flag Day in Banbury May 9, 1918 organised by the Early Closers War Fund Committee. In charge of the barrel organ were Pte's Seal and Oldhurst with Mrs G Stroud, Miss H Stroud, Miss E Stroud, Master H Stroud and Miss F Webb. On this occasion they raised £7.12s.3d of a total of £63.10s.6d. The net sum of £61.19s was distributed thus: to the Horton Infirmary £20, the War Work Guild £10, Nursing Association £5, St Georges Association £8.8s.6d and the Tea, Tobacco Fund at the Banbury Red Cross Hospital £18.10.6d.

Barry Davis

One of the many Flag Days organised throughout the war in Banbury. This one in aid of our Russian allies (Russian Red Cross) Organised by the Banbury Early Closers War Fund Committee in 1917.

Barry Davis

Day with competitions for handsome prizes and the selling of emblems (flags) in the streets

The Banbury Early Closers were very active in the town raising £105 9 shillings 8 pence with the aid of a barrell organ for the VAD Hospital tea, tobacco and cigarette Fund. It should be noted that the Early Closers Association, during the war, raised £4,500 for refreshments, tea and tobacco for the troops due to Mr Hastings and his committee's unremitting hard work.

An Agricultural Sale for war charities held on the Horsefair in March 1917 raised £1400 and on August 1, 1918 'Aeroplane Week' took place in Banbury. Government investments to the sum of £50,000 were required to purchase twenty fighter planes. One of the highlights of this drive was the display of a captured German 'Albatross' plane in the Market Place. However the aircraft was kept in an enclosure to facilitate obtaining a fee from those who wished to see it.

Everyone was encouraged to do their bit for the war effort. New schemes were started such as the National Egg Collection for the Wounded. The object of which was to collect and deliver newly laid eggs free of cost to wounded servicemen. In 1917 Banbury donated 707 eggs to this worthy cause.

Children played their part too. One task set was the collecting of conkers, tons of which were sent to drying centres before being despatched for use in munitions production. Newspapers, rags, bottles, and metal were also collected to aid the war effort. These were forwarded to the Department of Salvage for processing. The 1st Banbury Scout troop took, over the then empty, Jenkinsons shop (now Marchant + Reid) and here they set up a waste paper depot. They collected together masses of paper and jumble which were sent off to various manufacturers and the money raised was given to the St Dunstans Society for blinded servicemen. In January 1918 their Christmas Collection for the Blinded Soldiers childrens fund had raised £33 13s.

As well as the work of the charity organisations financing the war became a vital role of the people. They already contributed much in direct income tax and indirectly through tax on such items as drink and tobacco. Now they were asked to invest yet more money in War Bonds and loans.

On October 12, 1916 National War Savings were started. This was a leading feature of the town's activities in connection with the war. By 1918 there were 22 War Savings Associations in Banbury. During the week ending December 15, 1917 the purchase of National War bonds in Banbury represented the sum of £4,045 against the impressive £9,625 of the previous week. Nationally, in a twelve month period from late 1917 until the Armistice War bonds raised over £1,000 million.

Certificates awarded to brother and sister Alfred and Clara Lampitt of Green Lane, Banbury in recognition of their part in providing comforts for soldiers and sailors of the British Empire.

K Northover

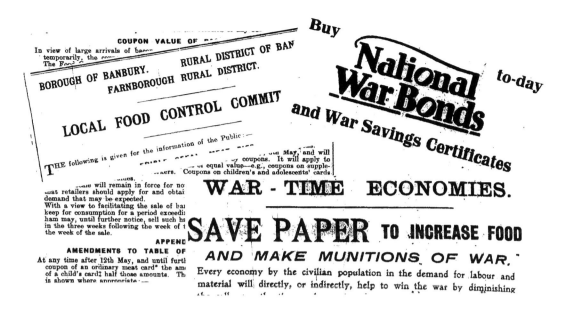

Rationing and Restrictions

When war was declared on Tuesday, August 4, 1914 an order in council was issued for the closing of banks for three extra days after the bank holiday. This resulted in a considerable shortage of money in the town but was necessary for the treasury to rush through the printing of new bank notes. Upon reopening gold sovereigns were called in and the first £1 notes and 10/- notes were issued.

There was some panic buying of food on Wednesday, some grocery shops shutting their doors at times during the day due to the overwhelming rush. Prices rose considerably, sugar doubled in price and cereals, bacon, butter, cheese and tinned and fresh meat all went up.

The Defence of the Realm Act (DORA) was introduced in August 1914. This gave the government extraordinary powers which were used with vigour as the months went on. Bank Holidays were cancelled, travel restricted, daylight saving was introduced and sporting occasions such as the Oxford and Cambridge boat race, horse racing and the football league were all suspended.

From 1915 public lighting was to be kept to a minimum, except those indespensible for public safety. These had to be shaded so as to be invisible from above as there was always the threat of attack from marauding zeppelins or bomber aircraft.

These restrictions during the winter evenings caused problems for pedestrians groping along in the dark. One anonymous Banburian wrote to the Banbury Guardian revealing the problems he had trying to find the letterbox at the Post Office and pleading for a small light to be installed. He wrote, 'after

FOOD CONTROL CAMPAIGN WEEK,

Commencing Monday, 4th June, 1917.

The National War Savings and Food Control Campaign Local Committee give Notice that a series of Meetings will be held as follows, viz. :

TUESDAY, JUNE 5th. at 7 p m.,
Dashwood Road Council Schools.
Neithrop (Boxhedge) Wesleyan Mission Hall.
Grimsbury—Christ Church Schools.

WEDNESDAY, JUNE 6th, 7 p.m.
Southam Road—Church of England Schools.
Cherwell Infants' Schools.

THURSDAY, JUNE 7th, 7 p.m.
Bridge Street—The Temperance Hall.
Globe Yard Mission Hall.

FRIDAY, JUNE 8th, 7 p.m.
The Peoples' Park—FINAL RALLY.

Food Control Campaign propaganda leaflet 1917.

Barry Davis

walking carefully up the pavement, feeling for the letterboxes, without success and colliding with several other people on a similar errand, I eventually tried to post my little handful of correspondence into the collar of a lady's dress!'

Lighting in shops was reduced, much to the annoyance of shop keepers and customers alike. In February 1916 Mrs Stroud, Grimsbury Green, of the well known family butchers wrote to her son George. 'We have had the weather very rough again but we must not mind that if it keeps the Zepp away. Banbury is in all darkness now, no lights to be seen. Will said that it is dreadful, the customers cannot tell what they are buying, whether it is mutton or pork. They can only have one light in the shop and blinds all down. I have had to get all dark curtains for our windows - what a bother this old Kaiser is to us all'.

Also under this new DORA regulation blackouts were implemented, car lights shielded and rear lights used and illuminated signs extinguished. Times for lighting vehicles and for obscuring of lighting was published in the local press. Any offender could be liable to six months in prison or a fine not exceeding £100 or both. To assist the depleted police force special constables were enrolled and patrolled the streets at night enforcing the blackout. They also undertook traffic control along with their other tasks.

Another restriction came into force at the beginning of 1916. The order was

BOROUGH of BANBURY

Aircraft Raids

Defence of the Realm Regulations.

The Public will please understand that the object of these Regulations is precautionary only and no unnecessary alarm need be felt by their publication.

In case of the appearance of hostile Aircraft the following signal will be given :

A series of short blasts of five seconds duration with five seconds interval between each blast will be sounded on the Hooter at the Works of Messrs. Samuelson & Co., Limited. No other signal is to be given.

The supply of Gas and Electricity will be cut off at the respective Works.

All other lights should be extinguished or darkened.

All persons should at once take refuge in cellars or the lowest rooms in the building.

It is most dangerous to remain in the streets.

The following Order has been made by competent Military Authority, and should be MOST STRICTLY OBEYED, as the penalties for breach of Regulations are severe :

Order of the General Officer Commanding-in-Chief, Southern Command, being a Competent Military Authority, issued under Regulation 12 of The Defence of the Realm (consolidation) Regulations, 1914, as to the reduction and extinction of lights in the Borough of Banbury.

1. In all brightly lighted streets and squares and on bridges a portion of the lights must be extinguished so as to break up all conspicuous groups or rows of lights, and the lights which are not so extinguished must be lowered or made invisible from above by shading them, or painting over the tops and upper portions of the globes : provided that while thick fogs prevail, the normal lighting of streets may be resumed.

2. Sky signs, illuminated fascias, illuminated lettering, and powerful lights of all descriptions used for outside advertising or for the illumination of shop fronts, must be extinguished.

3. The intensity of inside lighting of shop fronts must be reduced from one hour after sunset or earlier, if the Chief Constable of Police on any occasion so directs.

4. In all tall buildings which are illuminated at night, the greater part of the windows must be shrouded, but lights of a moderate brightness may be left uncovered at irregular intervals.

5. All lighted roof areas must be covered over, or the lighting intensity reduced to a minimum.

6. The lighting of Railway Stations sidings and goods yards, must be reduced to the intensity sufficient for the safe conduct of business there. The upper half of the globes of all arc lamps must be shaded or painted over.

7. Lights along the Water front must be masked to prevent as far as practicable the reflection of the light upon the water.

8. The lights of Omnibusses must not be more than is sufficient to enable fares to be collected, and must be obscured whilst crossing bridges.

9. The use of powerful lamps on motor and other vehicles is prohibited.

10. The aggregation of flares in street markets or elsewhere is prohibited.

11. In the case of sudden emergency, all instructions given by the Chief Constable of Banbury, as to the further reduction or extinction of lights shall be immediately obeyed.

12. This Order shall apply to the Borough of Banbury and, except where otherwise provided, to the hours betweet sunset and sunrise, and it shall remain in force during the war unless sooner revoked.

Banbury, 11th Feb., 1915.   *F. WILSON,* Chief Constable.

Air Raid Precautions Banbury 1915.
Oxfordshire County Council Photographic Archive

made by the liquor traffic control board created under the DORA in June 1915 to curb the excessive drinking in the transport, munitions and shipbuilding industries. Regulations were extended regarding the 'treating of drinks' . The non treating order meant that everybody had to pay for and drink their own purchase. Failure to comply could result in a fine. Opening hours for public houses and registered clubs had already been restricted by a previous order. With the large number of soldiers billeted in and around the town and the vital work of the filling factory this was generally welcomed in Banbury as a prudent measure.

With the increasing need by the military and vital services for fuel, petrol became rationed from August 1916 by an order in council leaving no provision for pleasure motoring. Reporting restrictions were also introduced on the press, censoring war news and forbidding the reporting of any information which was liable to cause alarm and despondancy.

As the new year dawned in 1917 the emphasis was on food. German submarines had been successful in sinking many of the merchant ships bringing supplies to England so the new Ministry of Food that had been set up in December 1916 began to encourage the cultivation of every spare piece of land available. Where possible unused plots in the town were to be dug and planted with vegetables. Banbury Co-operative Society were asked to open up more of their lands for allotments. Plans were made for breaking up of two or three acres of turf adjoining Hightown Road cottages and also on Grimsbury railway land. Later in 1918 during the potatoes planting campaign land was found at Boxhedge, Overthorpe and Broad Street.

The Banbury Gardeners Improvement Association had been formed and met at the White Horse Hotel. There lectures were given on subjects such as seed economy and treatment of soil etc.

As restaurants began to almost disappear and food queues grew to huge proportions the government attempted to impose a voluntary scheme of food rationing of bread, meat and sugar. This proposal of February 1917 was even taken up by the King who restricted himself to the voluntary ration and authorised a proclamation urging the public to practice good food economy. It was suggested that every person should restrict themselves to 4lb of bread, $2^1/_2$lb of meat and $^3/_4$lb of sugar each week.

As food economy became a case of extreme urgency a Food Economy Campaign Committee was set up in the town consisting of the following members; Ald W J Bloxham (Chairman), Councillor Whitehorn, Councillor Broadbank, Rev P Chalk, Mrs Fox, Mrs Bowkett. Miss Pearce, Miss Meyer, Mr R Martin, Mr R Luscombe, Mr W Smith, Mr F Knights, Mr H A Hodson, Mr G H Osborne, Mr W G Mascord (Carpenters & Joiners Society) Mr A Gillett (Amalgamated Engineers), Mr Jabez Webb (Co-op Society) and Mr H A Butler (Organising Secretary).

In January 1918 appeals for food economy were even being made in churches throughout the town, residents were encouraged in the keeping of pigs,

Ald W J Bloxham, Chairman of the Banbury Food Economy Campaign Commitee (right). Mr H A Butler, Organising Secretary (left).

Banbury Advertiser

poultry, rabbits and bees. However compulsory rationing was inevitable and by mid January a local rationing scheme was approved by the now Banbury Food Control Committee headed by the Chairman, Councillor Whitehorn. This would restrict the consumption of meats and certain dairy products.

On March 25 compulsory rationing came into force, forms of application for food cards were issued by the local Post Office to every household. These were duly filled in and returned to the food offices at 10 Broad Street, later at the Town Hall, whereupon ration cards were issued. One card for meat and bacon and one for butter, cheese and margerine. Each holder had to register with a butcher and a grocer so as to receive the ration of 15 ozs of meat, 5 ozs of bacon and 4 ozs of butter or margarine each week. ration books took the place of cards in October 1918.

The latter part of 1917 saw the establishment of communal kitchens throughout the country. These were the forerunners of the Second World War British Restaurants and were founded to provide a cheap substantial meal and also aid in the teaching of food economy. In Banbury Mr Ernest Samuelson placed the Britannia Works Library at the disposal of the town rent free. It was proposed that soups and puddings should be available six days of the week and joints and vegetables three times a week. A cook was to be appointed and volunteers found to serve.

At 2 o'clock on Saturday, January 19, 1918 the Communal Kitchen was opened to the public by Councillor Whitehorn. The Gas Company had placed two large cookers in the building free of charge. There were in addition two boilers, a draining board, sink, and utensils. Mrs Hallit had been appointed as cook and a number of ladies were secured to serve and prepare the first hun-

National ration book dated October 29, 1918 issued under the government Rationing Order of 1918. It contained coupons for meat, butter, margerine, sugar, lard and tea.

K Northover

dred meals expected to be sold daily. A sum of £35 was advanced by the Food Control Committee for initial expenses and a similar sum was raised as a guarantee fund, both amounts to be repaid if successful. Upon opening the kitchen was serving, on average 150 meals per day. Soup was available at 2d per pint, puddings 1d per portion and a mixture of various main meals such as toad in the hole 2d, shepherd's pie 2d with greens at 1d and potatoes boiled or mashed for 1d.

By mid 1918 Britain had established a system of control over nearly everything eaten and drunk by 40,000,000 people. The civilian population was now catered for like an army, nothing being left to chance.

The 'Fine Lady upon a white horse' in front of the Cross. Peace celebrations in Banbury in 1919.
Barry Davis

Peace Rejoicings at Banbury

News of the Armistice of November 11, 1918 was met with some trepidation. However, with the peace finally signed on June 28, 1919, Banbury could at last celebrate.

Banbury Peace Festival took place on Saturday, July 19, 1919 but was marred by rain which started some half an hour into the proceedings and continued throughout the day and night.

The event opened with the peal on the bells of the Parish Church at 7 am. The first item on the agenda was the procession. As early as 10 am large crowds

VAD Nurses and the Juvenile Foresters form up in preparation to join the Peace Parade in Banbury in 1919.

K Northover

assembled in South Bar where, already, the three mounted marshalls Lt Col Stockton, Major E C Fortescue and Lt I Stockton were busy placing every organisation in its correct order. The procession originally timed to start for 10.30 finally set off at 10.50 from St Johns Road, Crouch Street and Dashwood Road and was lead by two mounted Borough constables, Pc Hirons and Pc Kirk. Immediately behind came the band of the Comrades of the Great War in khaki pounding out the strains of patriotic songs. Next came a detachment of Northumberland Fusiliers with the ex-servicemen under Lt Harry Askew.

The Voluntary Aid Detachments car with its nurses and men was a reminder to all of the sterling work carried out by the station and hospital throughout the long campaign. Here Dr Beattie headed the group of nurses proudly marching along. After came the women land workers and a new group in Banbury, the Girl Guides commanded by Miss Meadows, Fairfax and Hankinson. These followed by the postal and telegraph services and the Oddfellows in their decorated car featuring 'Faith' 'Hope' and 'Charity"

The Courts of the Ancient Order of Foresters had made a combined effort with that of the Prince of Wales Court being represented by a young girl, Miss Leatherbarrow, on a white pony flanked by four horsemen in the green of Robin Hoods Sherwood Foresters. The Court Queen Mary had a decorated car followed by children on ponies, two boys with greyhounds on leashes then a large banner carried by members of the various courts. Thereafter came the members of an order even more ancient, the Independent Order of Rechabites dedicated to the pursuit of temperance, ironically followed a few places back by the 'Brewers' car with the bags of hops and barrels.

Following the Rechabites was the car of the Munitions Works No 9 (Banbury) Filling Factory. This was surmounted by representations of hand grenades, a gas shell charging machine and dozens of shells. As escort were smart looking girl munitions workers in uniform with the factory Fire Brigade. The Banbury Aviation Company not only sent a decorated lorry laden with girl workers but also a large model of a Sopwith Camel machine 'piloted' by Master Weston, son of the manager of the works. This popular exhibit caused some difficulty due to its size, in manipulating it through the streets. It was therefore excluded from the narrow Parsons Street.

The Banbury Fire Brigade followed with an ancient appliance of the 1830's flanked by equally ancient looking operatives. Then the modern brigade manned by Captain Fortescue, Sub Captain Thomas and Lt. Kilby. Part of the Fire Brigade's display was a decorated car featuring the figure of Britannia complete with trident (Miss Bustin) flanked by a juvenile soldier and sailor and bringing up the rear, the motor steamer. The Boy Scouts under Scoutmaster Robeson made an appearance. The *Banbury Guardian* car gave a practical exhibition of printing and distributing the Order of Procession from a hand printing press. Also to be seen on board was the latest monotype keyboard for typesetting and an older compositor. The Church Lads Brigade with Bugle Band then swinging into sight under Captain Webb and then the Early Closers car made an appearance. The highly decorated vehicle carried a number of wounded and disabled soldiers. The Wilts Dairy Company made an excellent show with their car stressing the importance of dairying and agriculture to the country. On display were cheese making equipment under the direction of Miss Lauder from Somerset and Miss Salter of Banbury. Milk was sold en route with the proceeds going to the Horton Infirmary.

There was a good attendance by the Star Cyclists Club after which came the Banbury Co-operative Society's car nicely decorated. Then the Borough band heralded the appearance of Miss Ruby Bradshaw as Banbury's famous Lady on a white horse with two grooms leading the white Arab charger, (a veteran of the battle of Mons in 1914), flanked by two mounted attendants, Miss C Bradshaw and Miss M Stockton. The 'Lady' wore a dress of rich white and gold brocade with bells on her toes. The attendants in black satin and silk costumes with large picture hats all of the restoration period.

A detachment of the 2nd Volunteer Battalion Oxon & Bucks Light Infantry under Captain Potts, with Captain E A Ffoulkes acting as rearguard formed the Mayoral escort when his worship joined the procession.

The route taken by the pageant was South Bar, Horsefair, Parsons Street, Market Place, Bridge Street, Middleton Road, West Street, North Street, East Street, Middleton Road, and Bridge Street. On the return journey the mayor

The Wiltshire Dairy Company's lorry which took part in the Peace Festival procession.

B Davis

and Corporation, Sir Rhys Williams, MP and the Borough officials joined the cavalcade at the Town Hall and proceeded up the High Street followed by a large crowd to the People's Park. The procession took half an hour to cover the route and was warmly received by locals and sightseers lining the streets and watching from windows and balconies.

At the park entrance the procession was joined by the High Steward of the Borough, Lord North accompanied by the Hon Mrs Fitzgerald and Miss Rothe. Here a large square was formed around a temporary platform in the centre of the park for the official opening ceremony.

Despite the rain falling there was a sizeable crowd in attendance. The Mayor opened the proceedings by asking the Town Clerk to explain briefly the bequest of Mr G V Ball. This was that the late George Vincent Ball had given officials of the town a sum of money in trust for the purchase of land near the town as a park for recreational uses of all classes of the public on seven days a week from sunrise to sunset. It was to be ornamentally planted and laid out and thereafter be known as the 'Peoples Park'. The proviso was that the Mayor and corporation must undertake the care of his family vault in Banbury ceme-tery. Should they fail to comply then the funds would pass to the Horton Infirmary. The Mayor then addressed the crowd regarding the victory and the peace before calling on Lord North to open the park. This he duly performed adding that he hoped many generations of Banbury people would enjoy it and spend many happy hours there.

Alderman Brooks as Chairman of the Peoples Park Committee was asked to thank Lord North and he briefly explained how the land had been purchased. The Mayor then introduced the member of the Banbury Division Colonel Sir Rhys Williams, MP whom he had entertained at the Town Hall earlier in the day. Lord North then responded to their thanks and the Borough band closed the proceedings with the national anthem.

Due to the wet weather the children's treats had to be postponed but the foresight of the Childrens Committee saved the day by providing indoor activities at several locations on the town. There was approximately 3,000 children to cater for and provisions were supplied by local tradesmen. The Mayor's party toured the various centres where the children were assembled for tea and money was left for games and competitions that were to follow.

As the rain was still falling heavily at 6 pm it was decided to postpone the illuminated fete until Monday evening. However the cinemas were opened and the usual Saturday dance at the Church House was well patronised. Whilst many people just strolled the streets inspecting the decorations and preparations for the forthcoming fete the bells of the Parish Church continued to peal late into the evening.

Despite the disappointment of the rain spoilt programme on Saturday this was relieved by a fine Monday evening when Banbury continued this Festival. This took the form of an illuminated fete in the vicinity of the Cross. Practically the whole of the town turned out to wonder at the spectacle of the lights whilst the bands of the Borough and Comrades provided the music. Large posts had been erected about a dozen yards distant at the bottom of West Bar, in the Horsefair and in South Bar and to these were suspended lights, streamers and flags while six smaller poles similarly decorated gave an effective finish to the scheme. Streamers of lights hung from poles stretched from Crouch Street to the beginning of North Bar whilst Japanese lanterns and fairy lights festooned the churchyard of the Parish Church. The porch of the Church House was illuminated with coloured electric lights as were most of the public buildings, gardens and private houses in the vicinity. Perhaps the most striking feature of all was the magnificent picture which the Cross presented, hundreds of electric globes had been used to outline the structure. In the dazzling glare of the red, white and blue lights the statues of Queen Victoria, her son and grandson glowed like white marble. Many noted the bare shield on which had been the German Royal Arms, which had been removed on Friday by order of the Mayor and officials of the town.

Many of the crowd engaged in dancing in the street to the music of the bands which provided as much amusement to those looking on as those taking part. A dance at the Church House attracted a good attendance where music was supplied by Miss Chiltons band. However much of the crowd just wandered in the street taking in the sights and enjoying reunions with friends and acquaintances. For most the evening seemed to pass too rapidly and the proceedings came to a close at eleven o'clock when the band struck up the national anthem. Even then the people continued to mill around the area and it was some time after before the streets were empty.

One other note on the programme was the firework display in People's Park at 10.30 pm. From well before 10 o'clock a large crowd had gathered and were rewarded by a fine display of rockets which darted into the sky, bursting into balls of gold, red, white and blue. Shortly the park became as light as day and the true size of the huge crowds was revealed. This was caused by the lighting of the 'Dover Flare' given by the admiralty from surplus stocks for use in peace celebrations. The flares had been used by the navy for illuminating the Dover straits during the war against enemy shipping. This burned for some ten minutes with a glare that could be seen for miles around a conclusion to a very memorable evening.

The next day, Tuesday afternoon saw the continuation of the childrens events with swimming competitions at the Corporation Baths, where the Mayor, Alderman Bloxham distributed prizes.

The childrens sports, postponed from Saturday took place on Wednesday. The venue for the event was at Durdans, Oxford Road (the old showground) at which some 3,000 scholars from the Elementary Schools attended and were joined by the Mayor and Mayoress.

Mr and Mrs Taylor of Calthorpe Street and their seven soldier sons. Their home at number 45 had a plaque placed over the door as they had the greatest number of sons serving. Back row Left to right Joe (ASC), Bert (RHG), Jess (1st/4th O&BLI), Dennis (1st/4th O&BLI), Harry (unknown). Front row Leo (1st/6th R War. Regt), Mr & Mrs Taylor, Fred (ASC). Note Dennis who died of wounds on the Somme in 1916 has been added by the photographer.

Mr D Solomon

War Shrines and Memorials

The Great War was uniquely tragic as a people's war, its effects reached every part of the nation, and the extent of grief was beyond any comprehension. The young men of a nation had left their homes, the farms and factories and were never seen again. The people had to find a way to mourn together, a form of recognition that no family was alone in its ordeal of sudden loss of those that they loved. Eventually this took the form of war memorials, which upon erection throughout the land gave terrible emphasis to the war's true extent. From The Cenotaph in Whitehall, London, to some tiny hamlet with its stone cross and half dozen or so names, the price of that conflict could not be more clearly realised.

The Roll of Honour of Banburians killed and wounded grew longer each week with details and photographs appearing in the local newspapers. In late

The White Comrade G. Hillyard Swinstead, R.I.
never lets a friend go under, but says — 'Lo I am with you alw'

Reprinted from "The Graphic" plate, by R. and T. Washbourne, Ltd.

The Great Sacrifice

" Greater love than this no man hath, that a man
lay down his life for his friends."
" I am the Resurrection and the Life."

As the advancement of the war brought greater suffering and loss, these cards were produced expressing
hope and redemption, that whatever happened, the salvation of God was always present.

K Northover

1916 War Shrines began to appear erected throughout the town. These shrines
of almost uniform design were a polished oak frame, glazed and enclosing a
list of names of the men who had fallen with the colours from the immediate
neighbourhood. Above the names were the words, 'God of all pity, Jesu blest -
grant them thy eternal rest'. The frame was surmounted by a simple cross and
at the base was a shelf and receptacle to accommodate floral tributes which
were meticulously cared for by local ladies. Later shrines had wings added
containing prints of contemporary paintings entitled 'White Comrade' and
'The Great Sacrifice'.

The service of dedication generally consisted of a procession from the local
church headed by a crucifix and surpliced choir followed by the clergy and
congregation. On reaching the site of the shrine the vicar would address the
crowd and hymns sung and prayers said.

Early in the war Calthorpe Street had the proud distinction of contributing
to the forces the largest proportion of men than any other street in the parish
and in acknowledgement the first shrine was provided and affixed to the
house of Mr & Mrs F Taylor at no 45. They had at this time sent six sons to the

Procession to the Calthorpe Street shrine.

Mr J Green

army, one having been killed in action and another being a prisoner of war. The shrine was of triptych shape. In the centre panel was the Roll of Honour bearing seventy-five names and beneath in a separate space headed-'The Heroic Dead' a list of eight names: H Taylor, W Simmonds, W R French, A Brain, W F Mobbs, J Jackson, E Armitt and D Taylor.

On the left wing of the memorial was a representation of the crucifiction with the words 'There stood by the Cross of Jesus, his Mother'. On the right wing a picture of the risen Christ with the text 'I am the resurrection and the life'. The shrines were manufactured by Messrs Hills and Rowney, in the Market Place.

The dedication took place on Sunday October 15, 1916, the service being conducted by the Vicar of Banbury, the Rev A J Jones, RD. This took place during an interval in the service of Matins at the Parish Church.

The procession consisting of the clergy, choir, congregation, Church Lads Brigade, Sunday School and a large number of the public making its way to Calthorpe Street by way of Horsefair and High Street. The vicar addressed the crowd, a hymn was sung and prayers said. The procession then reformed and made its way to the top of the street, moving into South Bar, then to Horsefair, finally re-entering the church.

On October 22, 1916 two war shrines were dedicated, one in Gatteridge

Street on the wall of the house of a Mr Maycock and the other on the corner of Windsor Street and Fish Street.

The Gatteridge Street Memorial bore at this time the names Frederick Charles Hazell, Bruce Swinton Smith Masters, George Arthur Smith Masters, Charles Tyrrell, Sidney Vicars Lester and Arthur Spafford. The Cherwell Street Shrine bore the names Edward Armstrong, William Pearson, Edwin Bedlow, Harold Prescott, Ernest Blencowe, Harold Carter, William French, Charles Hirons, Edward Whitlock and Albert Blencowe. This memorial's prints were donated by Mrs E Lamley Fisher and Mr C J Smedley.

The next shrine to be selected was placed on the wall of the house of Mr and Mrs Lovell at 19 East Street, Grimsbury. The Lovells had one son killed and another was missing. The names on the shrine were of men from East Street, Centre Street, North Street and South Street. They were William Powell, F Pickering, Mark Prue, William Lovell and Jack Wassall.

On Tuesday afternoon, November 4, 1916 three shrines were dedicated for the Neithrop district. The first was on the house of Mr Mold, Finlay Terrace, Warwick Road containing names of men from Warwick Road. The second on the house of Mrs Nutt, Boxhedge Square bearing the names of all the men from Boxhedge and Townsend district. The final shrine was on Mrs Clarke's house in Foundry Square for the men from that square, Bath Road, Southam Road and Foundry Street. These particular services attracted a crowd numbering some four to five hundred.

In early December the vicar of south Banbury and his congregation attended a service for a shrine which had been erected in Broad Street on the wall of the Fleur de Lys public house. The Roll contained forty names and had a central picture entitled 'For England' another shrine for the Cherwell Street area was fixed on the corner of the Britannia Works mechanic shop.

A further two shrines were dedicated by the Vicar of Banbury, on Sunday April 1, 1917. These war shrines had been placed in Bath Road and Southam Road. The former bore the name of those serving with the forces, those who had served and had now been discharged and those who had made the great sacrifice and whose homes were in the district of Bath Road, Bath Terrace, Queen Street, Park Road and Paradise Road.

The second mentioned bore a similar record of the men of the district of Southam Road, Castle Street, Factory Street and Compton Street.

The site for the war shrines in Bath Road was in front of Mrs Sturley's house. The list of three columns of those serving and five men who had laid down their lives including the names of four of Mrs Sturley's household, Those fallen were; James J Jackson, John Charles Bartlett, Wilfred Arthur Moss, John James Wheeler and Albert James Kilby.

The shrine in Southam Road was equally suitably sited, in the care of Mrs Watson who had two sons in the army, the youngest of whom was promoted to a commission from the ranks after further gallant service following the award of the Distinguished Conduct Medal. Following a long list of those serv-

The Neithrop War Memorial outside St Pauls
Church Warwick Road, Banbury.

J Northover

The War Memorial at Christ Church now situated in
St Leonards Church yard.

K Northover

ing came a list of thirteen dead; George Pulker, F Dumbleton, Eli Perrin, W J
Lidsey, William Alfred Harvey, Bertie Tims, Norman Shearsby, Harry Taylor,
Thomas E Taylor, Eli Upton, Frank Edward Turner, Frank Thornton and E A
Taylor.

There was a Roll of Honour on the Great Western Railway station platform
for many years and another on the wall of the General Post Office which can
still be seen today at its premises in the High Street.

Dedication of a Memorial Calvary at Christ Church, South Banbury.

An event of much interest to the town and particularly to those of the south
Banbury parish was the dedication by the Bishop of Oxford of a memorial in
honour of those who had fallen in the war which took place on the afternoon
of Tuesday, March 20, 1917 in the presence of a large crowd.

The Calvary, made of stone corresponding to that used in the building of
Christ Church, consisted of a pillar resting on large steps and surmounted by

a cross on which was the figure of Christ facing west and on the east side the figure of the Virgin and Child. It was situated in the enclosure at the north west corner of the church with the tower as the background.

The cost of the memorial had been covered by the subscription of over six hundred people amongst whom were some connected with the free churches of the town. The work had been entrusted by the architects, Messrs Scorer & Gamble of Lincoln to Messrs Bowman and Son of Stamford.

The structure of the stone, from Clipsham Quarry, was 15ft 3ins in height standing on a base with two steps of York stone slabs. The shaft consisted of one block of stone measuring 8ft 3ins. On one side was the Christ figure with the words below 'Greater love hath no man than this'. On the other side the Mother and Holy Child with the words 'God so loved the world that he gave his only begotten Son'. On the north side of the base was inscribed 'To the honour and glory of God. In loving and undying memory of the men who gave their lives in the Great War 1914- for God and King and Country'.

Rest eternal grant upon them O Lord and let light perpetual shine upon them'.

On the south side 'The nation writes their names on her Roll of Honour because they die for her; God writes them in his book of life because they die for him'.

The service of dedication in the Church commenced at five o' clock and there was a large congregation. Those conducting the service were the Vicar of Banbury and representatives from St Mary's, South Banbury and All Saints School, Bloxham. After the first hymn the Bishop addressed those present and the choir then gave a very effective rendering of the Russian 'Contakion of the faithfull departed', Kiev melody. The choir, clergy and Bishop then left the church in processional order followed by the congregation to the Calvary. The Bishop recited the words from the Burial Office and was followed by some responses and the Lords Prayer.

The unveiling of the memorial was by Seaman J G Robeson (who served the same gun as Jack Cornwall, VC at the Battle of Jutland) and Corporal A E Richer, Essex Regiment who was wounded at Beaumont Hamel on July 1, 1916. Then followed the dedication and final prayers. The Calvary survives and is now situated in the grounds of St Leonards Church, Middleton Road, Grimsbury.

Unveiling of the Neithrop Memorial.

A Cross erected in St Paul's churchyard and a tablet inside the church in memory of the Neithrop men who fell in the war were dedicated by the Archdeacon of Oxford on the afternoon of Sunday, October 24, 1920. The memorial, covered by the white ensign, was the work of Mr S Shirley. It consisted of a tall column of Portland stone on a plinth and two steps surmounted by a cross and bore the following inscription: '1914-18 To the glory of God and in memory of the men who gave their lives in the Great War',

"Grant them O God eternal rest and may light perpetual shine upon them',

'Greater love hath no man than this that a man lay down his life for his friends' (St John) A churchwarden, Mr C W Fortescue performed the unveiling.

The tastefully designed tablet on the south wall of the church was the work of Mr Blinkhorn and bore the names of 73 men and 1 nurse. The Union Jack covering it was removed by another churchwarden, Mr R F Horne.

The Banbury Peace Memorial.

After the peace of Versailles had been signed a suitable peace memorial was sought. It was decided to mark the occasion by improving and enlarging the Horton Hospital.

The hospital governors met on January 21, 1919 and decided to seek the approval of the people of Banbury. This done the Horton Peace Memorial Fund was established. Eventually a massive £25,000 was raised of which £10,000 was given by the British Red Cross Society.

The main needs of the hospital were for a nurses hostel (alone costing over £7,000 excluding furniture and fittings) new childrens ward, extensions for the existing male and female wards and a new kitchen and domestic quarters. On completion of these projects there would still remain funds for equipment including an X-ray machine costing in the region of £1,000.

A foundation stone laying ceremony took place in November 1920 by the Countess of Jersey, President of the Oxfordshire Red Cross, Lord North, the Banbury High Steward, Captain E Towse, VC (a blind South African War veteran) for the armed forces and Mr Alfred Turbitt for the Work People's Association.

The service of dedication was led by the Vicar of Banbury, Canon A J Jones. Amongst those represented at the service were civic dignatories, ex service men, nurses and hospital staff, scouts and guides, the Church Lads Brigade, firemen and police and members of local friendly societies and associations. Music was provided by the Banbury Borough Band and the band of the Comrades of the Great War.

St Mary's Church - The Banbury War Memorial.

Towards the end of 1921 an appeal was launched by the Parochial Church Council for donations for the St Mary's Church war memorial. The proposal was for the forming of a special chapel within the church and the placing of the roll of names of those who died in the war on panels.

It was estimated that the cost of founding the chapel would be £185 and £350 for the Roll of Honour. The work was duly approved and completed. On Saturday, November 11, 1922 at 2.30 pm, the anniversary of Armistice Day the

Rememberance Day, Banbury c1930.

Banbury Museum

unveiling and dedication of the oak tablets service was held at St Mary's Church. The memorial was designed by Mr Gilbert T Gardner LRIBA (Oxford) and the work was carried out under the direction of Mr W J Bloxham of Banbury.

The oak panels bore the names of 339 men and 1 woman from the borough who fell in the Great War and was situated in the south aisle of the parish church.

After the Second World War a further memorial was erected with the names of the dead of that conflict. This part of the church became known as the Chapel of Resurrection and in 1948 was dedicated to the dead of both World Wars.

The Cenotaph Peoples Park

On Sunday, September 14, 1919 despite unfavourable weather a memorial service for the fallen took place in the Peoples' Park attracting a very large attendance.

The service was inaugurated by the Banbury Branch of the Federation of Discharged Soldiers and Sailors and the Comrades of the Great War who accepted an invitation to take part in the gathering. Two hundred members of these bodies paraded in front of the town hall then joined by the Wesleyan band marched to the Peoples' Park by way of the High Street and West Bar, the procession being watched by crowds lining the streets. As the band and procession entered the park they halted in front of a temporary cenotaph guarded by men of the Northumberland Fusiliers, under Corporal Ross, who presented arms. One soldier stood at each corner with arms reversed while two stood, one either side of the cross with arms at the slope.

The memorial was in the form of a celtic cross about twelve feet high on which was inscribed at the base, 'To the sacred memory of the glorious dead'. A platform draped with the national colours had been erected in the centre of the park and immediately behind this the members of the Federation and the Comrades were lined up. By this time a large crowd had assembled and as the service was about to begin the rain began to fall, which unfortunately continued throughout. On the platform were the Rev A J Jones, (Vicar of Banbury), J E Smith-Masters (Vicar of South Banbury), J H French (Baptist), H G Godwin (Wesleyan), P Chalk (Unitarian) and A Lee. Also present were the Mayor Mr W J Bloxham, the deputy Mayor Councillor A E Fox and the Town Clerk Mr A Stockton.

Hymn sheets were distributed to those assembled and the Rev H G Godwin conducted the service. Thereafter followed the singing of hymns and recital of prayers and an address by the Vicar of Banbury.

During the final hymn a collection was taken for the Horton Infirmary Peace Memorial Fund. At the conclusion of the hymn the Vicar of Banbury pronounced the benediction and the 'Last Post', was sounded close to the cenotaph. With this the service was concluded. A large number of beautiful floral offerings were placed, amongst them was a large wreath from the Banbury Branch of the Federation and inscribed 'In memory of our fallen brothers'. The Comrades sent a wreath of laurel on which were the words 'God is gracious to the gallant men of England, gone west'. The memorial had been constructed and erected by Messrs. G F Braggins & Co and its construction and general appearance did the firm credit. At the base of the structure was an oak frame, with the list of the names of the fallen as compiled for the *Banbury Guardian*. The arrangements for the service were carried out under the superintendence of Mr Jordan, the president of the Banbury Branch of the Federation and Mr R H Prescott, the Secretary of the Comrades.

The Present Cenotaph

Prior to 1922 the temporary cenotaph in the Peoples' Park had marked Banbury's sacrifice in the Great War. A permanent memorial was required and several proposals were made. One not unlike the cenotaph in Whitehall was considered to be sited in the Horsefair opposite the parish church. This was however dismissed on the basis of such a large monument in such close proximity to Banbury Cross. The design eventually decided upon was a simple cross to be situated in Peoples' Park.

The public unveiling took place on St George's Day, Sunday, April 23, 1922. A large crowd of some 2000 people gathered under a dull April sky with storm clouds adding to a grave occasion. Poignantly, as the cross was unveiled a brilliant shaft of sunlight lit up the scene.

Prior to the unveiling a procession of military, ex-servicemen, public bodies and members of the corporation formed up in the Cow Fair at 2.30 pm, headed by the bugle band of the 4th Battalion Oxon & Bucks Light Infantry. The formation proceeded via High Street, West Bar and the Broad Shades to the Park. On arrival different organisations were drawn up to form three sides of a square facing the memorial. The fourth side composed the band, a platform for

Dedication of the temporary cenotaph in People's Park.

Banbury Museum

the service and special seats for relatives of the fallen. A ceremonial guard of Banbury Territorials was formed with two non commissioned officers and two men standing at the four corners of the memorial with bayonets fixed

The cenotaph designed by Mr Gilbert T Gardner IRIBA of Oxford and built by Mr T Cakebread took the form of a cross on a pedestal and base. On corresponding sides were the inscriptions 'Lest we forget The Great War 1914-18' and another setting forth that this Cross is erected to the memory of 325 men

The church ministers on the platform and the band.

B Davis

and one woman of Banbury who gave their lives in the Great War. The work was to be paid for by public subscription at an estimated cost of £300. When completed it had stone paving and surrounding metal fencing.

The service was conducted by local clergy headed by the vicar of Banbury. There followed the singing of hymns, reciting of prayers and verses and a sympathetic address by the Rev H G Godwin. Just before the unveiling Major-General Sir Francis Mulcaly, KCB addressed the crowd and in conclusion performed the lowering of the Union Jack from the cross at which point the territorial detachment presented arms in a general salute.

The Rev Canon Jones proceeded with a dedication 'In sacred memory of those who fell in the Great War', and this was followed by the placing of wreaths at the foot of the cross by relatives and public bodies. Amongst these were floral tributes from the Fire Brigade placed by Chief Officer Fortescue. One from the Girl Guides, the British Legion (Banbury Branch), The Banbury Harriers Athletic Club, VAD (Oxon), Banbury detachments 4th Oxon & Bucks Light Infantry, D Squadron Queens Own Oxfordshire Hussars, Oddfellows, and Banbury Early Closers Athletic Club.

The laying of wreaths was followed by the singing of a hymn, 'Oh Valiant Hearts' and the national anthem. The service was concluded by the 'Last Post' sounded by eighteen buglers of the 4th Battalion Oxon & Bucks Light Infantry and faintly from a distance was heard a cavalry reveille, symbolic of the transition from sleep to eternal life. A voluntary from the band saw the impressive ceremony draw to a close.

The permanent cenotaph in People's Park Banbury c1927.

K Northover

Memorial Certificate presented to the next of kin of those who fell. This one to Mrs G Bliss.

Centre for Banburyshire Studies

Roll of Honour

The Banbury Roll of Honour has been compiled from the list of names in St Mary's Church, the parish church. It records the names of those that died whilst serving in the various branches of the armed forces, or who died after discharge from wounds or illness, contracted whilst in uniform. The period covered is from August 1914 and appears to extend to the end of 1920.

The criteria for inclusion on the Roll is unclear but would normally include those resident in the town at the time of enlistment, or having been born or raised in Banbury. However, it is, clear that several, for some reason, have been omitted from the list. Most servicemen's details have been found through military records or the Commonwealth War Graves Commission but a few have remained untraceable

Number	Rank	Name	Born	Enlisted	Home Address	How Died	Where	Date	Batt/Regiment
65784	Pte 1	Akers, Rupert Eustace	Surbiton, Surrey	Guildford	13 West St	KIA	Salonica	28.11.16	RE (108 Fld Coy)
114004	Pte 2	Alexander, Frank, G	-	-	-14 Castle St	D	F+F	21.11.18	RE(HQ Signal Sect)
2659	Pte 3	Alexander, Percy	Neithrop	-Oxford	14 Castle St	DOW	F+F	12.2.16	1/4Oxf & Bucks LI
13019	Cpl 4	Allen, John Sydney	Castlefields, Shrews.	Shrewsbury	36 Britannia Rd	KIA	F+F	5.5.17	7 Shropshire LI
18753	Pte 5	Aris(s), Fredk. George	Banbury	Oxford	3 London Yard	DOW	F+F	18.10.15	5 Oxf & Bucks LI
201127	Pte 6	Ariss, Frank William	-	Oxford	37 Calthorpe St	DOD	F+F	22.9.18	2/4 Oxf & Bucks LI
11160	L/Cpl 7	Armitt, Edward	Banbury	Oxford	50 Calthorpe St	KIA	F+F	16.6.16	1 S Wales Borderers
-	Pte 8	*Armitt, G			50 Calthorpe St	-	-		Oxf & Bucks LI
8397	Sgt 9	Armitt, Thos W, DCM	Neithrop	Banbury	50 Calthorpe St	D	Mespot.	4.11.16	1 Oxf & Bucks
475106	Rfn 10	Armitt, George	Banbury	Banbury	50 Calthorpe St	KIA	F+F	24.9.18	12 London R 1746 O&BLI
28149	Pte 11	Allitt, Harold E	Banbury	Oxford	31 Union St	D	Home	15.2.20	1 Oxf & Bucks LI
_	Lt 12	Barton, John Charles	-	-	Oxford Rd	KIA	F+F	7.4.17	4 Oxf & Bucks LI
_	2nd Lt 13	Bidmead, Charles Hugh	-	-	Albert St	KIA	F+F	10.11.16	RFC GL + 25sq
_	2nd Lt14	Boast, Thos Townsend	-	-	20 Southam Road	K	F+F	29.9.18	3 Norfolk Reg
_	2nd Lt 15	Braggins, Albert Ed.	-	-	23 Marlborough Rd	KIA	F+F	29.4.18	7 Worcester R
200490	L/Cpl 16	Bannard, Percival Bryan	Deddington	Oxford	31 Southam Rd	KIA	F+F	7.8.17	1/4 Oxf & Bucks LI
202295	L/Sgt 17	Barnes, Albert	Churchill	Oxford	74 East St	KIA	F+F	22.8.17	2/4 Oxf & Bucks LI
J25742(D)Boy 1st class 18		Barnacles, Fredk. Andrew	-	-	Merton St	KIA	Coronel	1.11.14	RN HMS Monmouth
9199	Pte 19	Barnes, William A	Neithrop	Oxford	43 Cherwell St	D	Mespot.	10.7.16	1 Oxf & Bucks LI
8738	L/Cpl 20	Bartlett, John Charles	Banbury	Oxford	29 Queens St	KIA	F+F	1.8.16	2 Oxf & Bucks LI
56891	Gnr 21	Batts, William Fredk.	Chipping Norton	Oxford	12¹/₂ South Bar	KIA	F+F	30.3.17	RGA (57 Siege Bty)
297308	Gnr22	Bearsley, Fredk.	Banbury	Oxford	15 Beargarden	DOW	F+F	12.10.17	RGA(135 OHB)
498382	Pte 23	Beasley, Harry Walter	Kings Sutton	Aldershot	34 Broad St	KIA	F+F	25.4.18	RE (456 Fld Coy)
235035	Pte 24	Bedlow, Albert	Byfield	Derby	9 Paradise Rd	D	F+F	29.10.17	8 Suffolk Regt
18749	Pte 25	Bedlow, Edwin Richard	Banbury	Oxford	7 Jubilee Terrace	KIA	F+F	10.12.15	5 Oxf & Bucks LI
8532	Pte 26	Bigg, E Herbert-James	Bedford	Banbury	73 Merton St	DOW	F+F	22.10.14	2 Oxf & Bucks LI
-	2Lt 27	Blacklock, Algernon Haden	-		Overthorpe House	KIA	-	21.10.14	A & S Highlanders
23643	Pte 28	Blackwell, Thomas	Adderbury	Banbury	34 Fish St	DOW	F+F	25.9.17	6 Oxf & Bucks
200447	Pte 29	Blencowe, Albert	Banbury	Oxford	20 Boxhedge Sq	DOW	F+F	4.9.17	1/4 Oxf & Bucks LI
2494	Sgt 30	Blencowe, Alfred	Neithrop	Oxford	61 Upper Windsor St	DOW	F+F	16.8.16	1/4 Oxf & Bucks LI
10133	Pte 31	Blencowe, Ernest	Neithrop	Oxford	61 Upper Windsor St	KIA	F+F	5.8.15	5 Oxf & Bucks LI
9710	Pte 32	Bliss, Artie Charles	Banbury	Birmingham	37 Church Lane	KIA	F+F	25.9.15	5 Oxf & Bucks LI
28085	Pte 33	Bliss, Ernest Wilkins	Banbury	Banbury	37 Church lane	DOW	F+F	6.10.17	1 Somerset LI
156	Pte 34	Bliss, Frank Humphriss	Banbury	Birmingham	22 West Bar	KIA	F+F	23.7.16	14 R Warwick Regt.

Harry Dale

IN LOVING MEMORY OF

Pte. Harry Dale,

(First Somerset L. I. Late army A V. C.)

The dearly beloved eldest Son of Ernest & Susan Dale.

Who was killed in action in France March 30th, 1918.

Aged 26 Years.

———

Greater love hath no man than this,
That he lay down his life for his friends.

Memorial card for Pte Harry Dale, Somerset Light Infantry of Duke Street, Banbury.

K Northover

Somewhere in France there is a grave,
Where sleeps our soldier Son, amidst the brave,
No Mother or loved one to see die,
To kiss his dear face or say good-bye,
He bravely answered his country's call,
And gave his young life for one and all.

Of all the great poetry of the War these simple lines of a mother's words are as intense as any composed.

Number	Rank	Name	Born	Enlisted	Home Address	How Died	Where	Date	Batt/Regiment
4714	Pte 35	Bliss, Joseph	Banbury	London	107 West St	KIA	F+F	9.10.16	9 London Regt
201372	Pte 36	Blundall, Arthur Henry	-	Oxford	3 Grove St	KIA	F+F	23.7.16	1/4 Oxf & Bucks LI
273	Sgt 37	Boneham, Walter	Banbury	Banbury	The Shades, West Bar	KIA	F+F	8.5.15	1/4 Oxf & Bucks LI
4297	Pte 38	Bonner, Edwin Cyril	-	Oxford	High St, Adderbury	KIA	F+F	14.8.16	1/4 Oxf & Bucks LI
10298	Pte 39	Boscott, Charles	Banbury	Banbury	9 Foundry Square	KIA	F+F	25.9.15	2 Oxf & Bucks LI
7611	Pte 40	Boughton, Walter H	Bletchley, Bucks	Banbury	Merton St	KIA	F+F	31.10.14	2 Oxf & Bucks LI
10002	Pte 41	Boxold, Harry	Banbury	Banbury	69 High St	KIA	F+F	29.7.16	20th R Fusiliers
267728	Pte 42	Boyles, Frank	Banbury	Banbury	5 Castle St East	KIA	F+F	21.11.17	2/7 R Warwick Regt
8840	Pte 43	Braggins, Colin Frederick	Banbury	Oxford	23 Marlborough Rd	DOW	F+F	25.9.15	5 Oxf & Bucks LI
17083	Pte 44	Braggins, Charles	-	Northampton	4 Lower Cherwell St	DOW	F+F	19.10.17	6 Northampton Regt
1088	Cpl 45	Brain, Albert	Banbury	Coventry	56 Calthorpe St	KIA	F+F	21.11.14	2 R Warwick Regt
1327	Cpl 46	Brain, Tom	Neithrop	Banbury	15 Townsend	DOW	F+F	7.10.16	2/4 Oxf & Bucks LI
J34903(PO)	Boy 1 47	Brain, William Henry	-		Woodgreen	KIA	Jutland	31.5.16	RN HMS Indefatigable
871	Pte 48	Broughton, Ernest William	Banbury	Birmingham	34 West Bar	KIA	F+F	23.7.16	14th R Warwick Regt
200568	Sgt 49	Buller, Frank	Banbury	Oxford	32 North Bar	KIA	F+F	6.9.17	2/4Oxf & Bucks LI
18073	Pte 50	Buller, George Edward	Banbury	Oxford	32 North Bar	D		12.9.15	6 Oxf & Bucks LI
18754	Pte 51	Buller, Richard Thomas	Banbury	Oxford	32 North Bar	DOW	F+F	4.9.16	6 Oxf & Bucks LI
204401	Pte 52	Burdett, Thomas	Hawksbury Warks.	Coventry	Three Pigeons Southam Rd	DOW	F+F	30.3.18	1 Somerset LI
M2/149629	L/Cpl	Busby, Frank Thomas	Banbury	Banbury	White Horse Hotel High St	D		20.10.18	ASC MT 56 Mech. Trans. Coy.
863010	Pte 54	Butler, Sydney	-		4 High St	DOW	F+F	6.4.18	19 Bn Canadian Infantry
S/14243	Rfn 55	Baker, Thomas Henson	Banbury	Caversham (Berks)		KIA	F+F	21.11.17	10th Rifle Brigade
-	Gnr 56	✻Caisbrook, W G			Merton St	-	-	-	RHA
240340	Pte 57	Callow, William James	-	Oxford	16 Cherwell Terrace	KIA	F+F	22.8.17	2/4 Oxf & Bucks LI
9681	Pte 58	Carpenter, Bernard John	Neithrop	Banbury	43 Factory St	D	Mespot	30.1.17	1 Oxf & Bucks LI Q Coy
M2/100581	Pte 59	Carter, Alfred James	Oxford	Reading	20 Warwick Rd	-	F+F	4.4.18	RASC MT
22142	L/Cpl60	Carter, Frank	Banbury	Banbury	52 East St	KIA	F+F	22.8.17	5 Oxf & Bucks LI
19650	Pte 61	Carter, Harold	North Newington	Banbury	3 Upper Windsor St	KIA	F+F	31.8.16	6 Oxf & Bucks LI
106904	Pte 62	Castle, Albert	Grimsbury	Banbury	16 Bath Terrace	DOW	F+F	24.10.18	RAMC
25452	Pte 63	Castle, Frank	Milcombe	Abertilley, Glam.	Kings Rd	DOW	F+F	10.5.18	14 Worcester Regt
200053	Pte 64	Checkley, Charles Alfred	Banbury	Banbury	44 Castle St West	KIA	F+F	31.5.17	1/4 Oxf & Bucks LI
9227	Pte 65	Cherry, Richard	Banbury	Oxford	29 Union St	KIA	F+F	25.9.15	2 Oxf & Bucks LI
	Pte 66	✻Cherry, R			Factory St				Oxf & Bucks LI
T202293	Pte 67	Claridge, Alfred Amos	Banbury	Banbury	34 Calthorpe St	DOW	F+F	24.10.17	3/4 R West Surrey Regt
35284	Pte 68	Claridge, Frank	Banbury	Banbury	24 West Bar	D	Home	6.1.17	13th Devon Regt
3/9055	Pte 69	Clark, Horace William	Hook Norton	Middleton Cheney	5 Foundry Square	KIA	F+F	28.10.15	5 Northants Regt
9833	Pte 70	Clarke, William Alexander	Grimsbury	Northampton	84 West St	DOW	F+F	29.10.14	2 Bedford Regt
G/24595	Pte 71	Clarke, Reginald Hingley	North Wales	Banbury	11 Compton St	KIA	F+F	12.10.17	7 R West Kent Regt
200577	L/Cpl 72	Clements, James Gilkes	Grimsbury	Oxford	52 East St	KIA	F+F	3.5.17	5 Oxf & Bucks LI
71986	Pte 73	Clutterbuck, George	Banbury	St Helen's Lancs	Springfields	KIA	F+F	1.5.17	RGA (24 HB)
207269	Cpl 74	Coates, Stanley George	Banbury	Kings Lynn	9 South Bar	D	Home	21.12.18	3 Worcester Regt
27974	Pte 75	Coleman, Thomas	Grimsbury	Banbury	8 Duke St	KIA	F+F	21.3.18	2/4 Oxf & Bucks LI
	Pte 76	✻Compton, Leonard			37 Factory St				1/4 Oxf & Bucks LI
9680	Pte 77	Compton, Thomas Henry	Banbury	Oxford	37 Factory St	DOW	F+F	25.9.15	2 Oxf & Bucks LI
41483	Pte 78	Compton, Thomas H	Banbury	Banbury	23 West Bar	KIA	F+F	24.4.18	6 R Berks Regt
200918	Pte 79	Compton, William James	Banbury	Banbury	37 Factory Street	KIA	F+F	16.8.17	1/4 Oxf & Bucks LI
9772	Pte 80	Cooper, Joseph James	Banbury	Banbury	6 Lower Windsor St	DOW	F+F	18.5.15	2 Oxf & Bucks LI
35846	L/Cpl 81	Cooper, James William	-	Oxford	6 Lower Windsor St	KIA	F+F	23.8.18	14 R Warwick Regt
-	2nd Lt 82	Coulthard, Eustace Frank	-	-	10 West St	KIA	Mespot	6.4.16	9(1st)Oxf & Bucks LI
242589	Pte 83	Creed, John	Banbury	Banbury	40 Castle St East	DOW	Home	28.2.18	1/6 R Warwick Regt
200590	Pte 84	Cull, Alfred	Wilts	Oxford	12 Albert St	KIA	F+F	13.8.16	1/4 Oxf & Bucks LI
21055	Pte 85	Curtis, George Edward	-	Banbury	1 Shades West Bar	DOW	F+F	23.8.18	2 Oxf & Bucks LI
13027	A/Sgt 86	Caisbrook, James Henry	Clifton, Worcs	Kingston-upon-Thames	Sutton, Surrey	KIA	F+F	27.7.17	13th East Surrey
23697	Pte 87	Cleaver, Walter Clement	Banbury	Banbury		KIA	F+F	21.3.18	2/4 Oxf & Bucks LI
-	Lt 88	Drake, Francis			7 Albert Terrace	KIA	F+F	27.3.18	West Yorks Reg. (Att 2/4 KOYLI)
37921	Pte 89	Dale, Harry Reuben	-	Worcester	22 Duke St	KIA	F+F	30.3.18	1 Somerset LI
3154	Cpl 90	Davies, Sydney John	Banbury	Grimsbury		KIA	F+F	26.6.16	3 Coldstream Gds
11884	Pte 91	Denton, Horace Richard	Northants	Rugby	Plough Inn	KIA	F+F	14.4.16	6 Oxf & Bucks LI
53624	Staff Sgt 92	Denton, James Samuel	-		Plough Inn	D	Home	13.2.19	RGA
203164	Pte 93	D'Oyly, Christopher Henry	-	-Oxford	116 Middleton Rd	KIA	F+F	23.3.18	5 Oxf & Bucks LI
32102	Pte 94	D'Oyly, Thomas William	Banbury	Banbury	51 Kings Road	KIA	F+F	22.3.18	7 Somerset LI
5656	L/Cpl 95	Dudley, William Henry	Grimsbury	Oxford	84 Middleton Road	KIA	F+F	15.9.16	21 London R
505837	Spr 96	Dumbleton, Charles Thomas	-		Previously 5-6 Southam Road	DOW	F+F	3.10.18	Canadian Eng. 10th Bn
260059	Pte 97	Dumbleton, Earnest William	Banbury	Bedford	Previously 5-6 Southam Road	KIA	F+F	19.7.17	5 Yorkshire Regt.
L/8112	CSM 98	Dumbleton, F	Oxford	Canterbury	11 Castle St West	KIA	F+F	18.8.16	8 East Kent Regt.
306326	Pte 99	Dearlove, George William Dix	Banbury	Aston, Birm.	Grimsbury	DOW	F+F	25.10.18	2/7 Royal War. Regt
73324	Pte 100	Eaglestone, Ronald Henry	Bristol	Northampton	Bird in Hand	DOW	F+F	23.8.18	10 Notts & Derby Regt
108283	Gnr 101	Eaves, Harry	Banbury	Cowley	20 Broad St	D	Home	2.3.17	Wessex RFA
9329	Pte 102	Eden, Fredrick	Neithrop	Oxford	9 Boxhedge Sq	KIA	Persian Gulf	22.11.15	1 Oxf & Bucks LI
8966	Pte 103	Eden, Job	Neithrop	Banbury	9 Boxheadge Sq	D	Mespot.	6.10.16	1 Oxf & Bucks (S Coy)
L/10538	Pte 104	Eden, Percy Alfred	Banbury	Bexhill, Sussex	9 Boxheadge Sq	DOW	F+F	17.5.16	2 R Sussex Regt
142511	Pte 105	Edwards, George Edward	-		1E Old Grimsbury Rd	D	Home	11.1.19	RAMC
15349	Pte 106	Fairfax, Fred	Banbury	Oakham	Causeway	DOW	F+F	30.11.17	1 Coldstream Gds.
59282	Pte 107	Fox, Dennis	Shennington	Banbury	Castle St. West	D	F+F	22.4.17	9th Inf Lab Coy Devonshire Regt
18736	Pte 108	Franklin, William John Walter	-		10 Southam Rd	KIA	F+F	28.4.17	1 Royal Marines
3266	Bglr109	French, Joseph W	Neithrop	Banbury	19 Monument St	KIA	F+F	6.6.15	Rifle Brigade
8905	Sgt 110	French, William Robert	Banbury	Banbury	13 Southam Rd	KIA	F+F	16.5.15	2 Oxf & Bucks LI
9677	Pte 111	French, William	Bethnel Green, Middx	Oxford	5 Factory St	DOW	F+F	10.5.15	2 Oxf & Bucks LI
268187	Pte 112	French, William George	Banbury	Banbury	12 Bath Terrace	DOW	F+F	3.10.18	RE GHQ Wireless Grp
18740	Pte 113	French, Sydney			Upper Heyford	D	Home	-	2 Leicester Regt
85777	Pte 114	Friend, Henry Victor	Gt Tew	Banbury	West Bar	KIA	F+F	6.10.18	2/6 Durham LI
265389	Bglr 115	Fell, Christopher William	Banbury	Aylesbury	20 Globe Yard	KIA	F+F	10.3.17	1st/1st Bucks Bn Oxf & Bucks LI
350414	Pte 116	Ford, Frederick Charles	Banbury	Banbury	51 Bridge St	KIA	F+F	12.10.18	9 th HLI
-	Adj/Capt 117	Griffin, Innes Edward	-	-	Danvers House	DOW	F+F	19.2.16	4 Oxf & Bucks LI
53233	Pte 118	Gardiner, William Richard	Banbury	Banbury	66 Bridge Street	KIA	F+F	16.4.17	20 R. Fusiliers
155404	Pte 119	Garnett, Roland	Preston, Lancs	Banbury	91 High Street	KIA	F+F	24.9.18	MGC
5178	Pte 120	Gaunt, Percy	Oxford	Banbury	83 Causeway	KIA	F+F	19.11.16	1/4 Oxf & Bucks LI
220062	Pte 121	Gillett, William Pilgrim	Banbury	Banbury	Windsor Street	DOW	F+F	24.3.18	2 R Berks Regt
93779	Pte 122	Gillett, James Arthfrd	Banbury	Banbury	79 Causeway	DOW	F+F	17.7.17	Labour Corps.
285722	Pte 123	Gillett, Leonard George	-	Oxford	78 Causeway	D	F+F	20.5.17	QOOH (Oxford Yeomanry)
4877	Pte 124	Gibbard, George	-	Oxford	32 Foundry Square	DOW	F+F	19.7.16	2/8 R Warwicks LI
9008	Pte 125	Gibbard, Tom	Neithrop	Banbury	32 Foundry Square	KIA	Persn Gulf	22.11.15	1 Oxf & Bucks LI
34759	Sgt farrier 126	Gibbard Horace	Banbury	Lincs	19 Broughton Road	KIA	F+F	9.4.17	RFA (71st Brigade C Batt)
9552	Pte 127	125 Giles, Walter Charles	Banbury	Oxford	Neithrop	KIA	F+F	1.12.17	6 Oxf & Bucks LI
F/2034	Sgt 128	Gilkes, Charles T	Banbury	Birmingham	35 Causeway	DOW	F+F	4.10.16	23 Middlesex Regt

The original wooden grave marker of 4877 Pte George Gibbard, Royal Warwickshire Regiment who died of wounds at No 44 Casualty Clearing Station, France on July 19, 1916.

K Northover

Number	Rank	Name	Born	Enlisted	Home Address	How Died	Where	Date	Batt/Regiment
M2/046064	Pte 129	Gilkes, Harold, Daniel	-	-	68 Fish Street	D	Home	30.12.18	ASC (MT)
21318	Pte 130	Golby, Ernest	Banbury	Birmingham	43 Causeway	KIA	Italy	15.6.18	1/4 Oxf & Bucks LI
T205151	Pte 131	Green, Charles Henry	Banbury	Middlesex	5 North Bar	KIA	F+F	26.10.17	R W Surrey
P/4362	Pte 132	Green, William Tom	Radway	Banbury	3 Townsend	DOW	F+F	2.9.16	11 Rifle Brigade
292568	Gnr 133	Gregory, Charles Percy	Banbury	Banbury	86 Warwick Road	KIA	F+F	11.8.17	RGA 135 OHB
28675	Pte 134	Godfrey, George Alderman	Banbury	Banbury	38 North Bar	KIA	F+F	15.10.17	6 Somerset LI
50716	Pte 135	Godfrey, Henry Thomas	Banbury	Oxford	38 North Bar	KIA	F+F	24.8.18	1 R. Berks Regt
126545	Pte 136	Goodwin, John Christopher	-	-	1 Monument Street	KIA	F+F	10.8.18	Canadian Infantry 44 Bn
19611	Pte 137	Grimsley, Walter Charles	Banbury	Banbury	36 Church Lane	KIA	F+F	7.6.15	Wiltshire Regt.
9942	Pte 138	Gunn, James	-	Oxford	11 West Bar	D	Home	13.2.17	Oxf & Bucks LI (Depot)
203378	Pte 139	Garrett, Alfred	Banbury	Oxford	Chilvers Coton, Warks	DOW	F+F	11.8.18	2/4 R Berks Regt.
22414	Pte 140	Garrett, David	Banbury	Warwick	Longford, Coventry	DOW	F+F	23.12.17	16 R Warwick. Regt.
-	2Lt 141	Garside, Jack	-	-	-	Acc. Killed	Home	18.11.18	RAF
45423	Pte 142	Green, James Henry	Kennington, Surrey	Oxford	-	KIA	F+F	29.8.18	2 R. Berks Regt.
-	Capt 143	Hunt, Robert Lancelot Gibbs	-	-	46 The Green	KIA	F+F	7.10.16	6 Oxf & Bucks LI
702546	Pte 144	Hambridge, Harry	Banbury	Oxford	5 Windsor Street	KIA	F+F	15.10.18	23 London Regt.
263101	Pte 145	Hamer, William Sydney A	Banbury	Banbury	Fairview, Prospect Rd	KIA	F+F	29.8.18	2/4 R W Riding Regt.
2748	Pte 146	Harris, George	Banbury	Oxford	24 Crouch Street	DOW	F+F	13.7.15	1/4 Oxf & Bucks LI
37192	Pte 147	Harris, Harry Thomas	Banbury	Banbury	108 Warwick Rd	KIA	F+F	18.9.18	7 Norfolk Regt
19898	Pte 148	Harris, James Walter Thomas	Stratton Audley	Oxford	5 Castle St. North	D	F+F	12.10.18	MGC, Formrly Ox & Bucks
51892	Pte 149	Harrison, Alfred Abram	Burton Dassett	Rugby	Grimsbury	KIA	F+F	29.7.16	RE 87 Field Coy.
47072	Pte 150	Hartwell, Henry Charles	Banbury	Banbury	10 New Rd	KIA	F+F	15.10.18	1 R Innisk. Fusiliers
21012	Pte 151	Hartwell, Ralph Oliver	Banbury	Devizes	10 New Road	KIA	F+F	9.8.18	2 Wiltshire Regt.
10289	Pte 152	Harvey, William Alfred	Banbury	Oxford	2 Southam Rd Court	KIA	Gallipoli	27.5.15	4 th Worcester Regt
43888	Cpl 153	Hassell, John	-	-	-	Died	Home	-	QOOH /5th Cav Res
20848	Pte 154	Hazell, Frederick Charles	Woburn Green, Bucks	Banbury	21 Albert St	KIA	F+F	24.8.16	6 th Oxf & Bucks LI
-	Pte 155	Hearn, Robert Nicholas	-	-	85 Merton St	D	Home	29.4.15	1/4 Oxf & Bucks LI
182564	Gnr 156	Heritage, Arthur Horace	Banbury	Banbury	59 Queens St	KIA	F+F	23.9.18	RGA
3257	L/Cpl 157	Hirons, Charles Frederick	-	Oxford	4 Fish St	DOW	F+F	16.8.16	1/4 Oxf & Bucks LI
17372	Pte 158	Hitchcox, Eric	Warwicks	Banbury	32 Calthorpe St	KIA	F+F	31.3.16	6 Oxf & Bucks LI
15652	Pte 159	Hitchcox, Herbert	Wroxton	Oxford	32 Calthorpe St	KIA	F+F	25.9.15	10 Gloucester Regt.
131861	Pte 160	Hoare, Charles	Banbury	Banbury	Castle St East	KIA	F+F	4.5.18	MGC
201275	Pte 161	Hobbs, Arthur James	-	Oxford	28 Crouch St	KIA	F+F	9.6.17	2/4 Oxf & Bucks L I
177937	Pte 162	Hobbs, Norman Cyril	-	Oxford	28 Crouch St	DOW	F+F	4.11.17	RFA
17784	Pte 163	Hobbs, William Albert	Banbury	Oxford	17 Foundry Sq	D	Home	6.6.15	3 Garrison Oxf & Bucks
110241	Gnr 164	Hodges, Charles Harry	Bridgewater	Stratford-on-Avon	-	KIA	F+F	23.7.17	RGA 244 Siege Battery
-	Cpl 165	Hodgkins, George Thomas	-	-	93 West St	D	Home	10.3.18	Oxf & Bucks LI
27316	L/Cpl 166	Honeysett, Bertram Thomas	Surrey	Banbury	25 Horsefair	D	F+F	8.9.18	RE 'L' 2 Signal Coy
88479	Pte 167	Hopkins, John William	Oxford	Banbury	98 West St	KIA	F+F	1.9.18	6 Liverpool Regt.
8494	Pte 168	Horley, Frederick	Bloxham	Rugby	-	KIA	F+F	28.1.15	4 KRRifle C
201599	Pte 169	Howe, William	-	Oxford	37 Townsend	KIA	F+F	16.9.17	1/4 Oxf & Bucks LI
22649	Pte 170	Humphris, Frederick	Banbury	Oxford	83 Merton St.	KIA	F+F	3.9.16	6 Oxf & Bucks LI
-	Pte 171	*Humphris, George Henry W	-	-	12 Lower Windsor St	-	-	-	-Oxf & Bucks LI
200579	L/Cpl 172	Humphris, Richard	St Lukes, Middx	Oxford	Warwick Rd	KIA	F+F	13.8.16	1/4 Oxf & Bucks LI
200190	L/Cpl173	Hutchings, George Edwin	Banbury	Banbury	43 Calthorpe St	KIA	F+F	28.4.17	2/4 Oxf & Bucks LI
1436	Sgt 174	Hyde, Charles Frederick John	Banbury	Banbury	18 Castle St, West	KIA	F+F	27.4.15	QOOH

Number	Rank	Name	Born	Enlisted	Home Address	How Died	Where	Date	Batt/Regiment
8489	Pte 175	Huckins, Eric William	Banbury	Banbury	10 Southam Rd	KIA	F+F	16.5.15	2 Oxf & Bucks LI
33042	Pte 176	Hucklebridge (Jack) Henry	-	Aylesbury	3 Castle St North	KIA	F+F	7.10.16	6 Oxf & Bucks LI
202208	Pte 177	Hands, John	Aynho	Banbury	-	KIA	Italy	15.6.18	1/4 Oxf & Bucks LI
201864	Pte 178	Impey, Harry	-	Oxford	2 Britannia Rd	KIA	F+F	22.8.17	2/4 Oxf & Bucks LI
6808	Pte 179	Jackson, John	Neithrop	Gosport	53 Calthorpe St	DOW	F+F	27.10.14	2 Oxf & Bucks LI
9470	Pte 180	Jackson, James George	Banbury	Middleton Cheney	62 Kings Rd	KIA	F+F	16.9.14	1 Northampton Regt
24326	Pte 181	Jarvis, Arthur Andrew	Banbury	Banbury	Fish St	KIA	F+F	13.11.16	2 Oxf & Bucks LI
200778	Pte 182	Jelfs, Ernest Charles	-	Oxford	30 Parsons St	KIA	F+F	16.8.17	1/4 Oxf & Bucks LI
306733	Pte II 183	Jennings William Henry Southwood	Taunton, Somerset	-	19 Gatteridge St	Acc Killed	Home	8.11.18	RAF Recruits Training Wing
17783	Pte 184	Jones, John William	Northants	Mkt Harborough	41 Middleton Rd	D	F+F	3.9.17	Coldstream Guards
-	Lt 185	Jones, Thomas Lewis, MC	-	-	23 Albert St	DOW	F+F	10.10.18	8 Worcester Regt.
G78928	Pte 186	Jordan, Fredk Frank	Banbury	Banbury	5 Grove St	KIA	F+F	22.8.18	1/22 London Regt.
G/9820	Pte 187	Justice, William John	Banbury	Surrey	124 Causeway	KIA	F+F	7.6.17	10 West Surrey Regt.
116561	Pte 188	Jones, Ernest Robert Percy	Worcester	Camberwell	19 Compton St	DOW	F+F	20.5.18	RAMC 46 Stat Hosp
17861	Pte 189	Kennedy, Frank Hamilton	Banbury	London	50 Centre St	KIA	F+F	16.1.17	1 Grenadier Guards
-	2Lt 190	King, Harold Dudley	-	-	12 North St	KIA	F+F	6.10.18	1/8 Worcester Regt.
19746	Pte 191	Kinnerley, Arthur Charles	Banbury	Oxford	4 Cherwell St	KIA	F+F	3.9.16	6 Oxf & Bucks LI
9247	Cpl 192	Kilby, Albert James	Neithrop	Banbury	57 Kings Rd	KIA	F+F	30.7.15	5 Oxf & Bucks LI
200603	Sgt 193	Kilby, Herbert	Fritwell	Oxford	County Police Stn	KIA	F+F	28.4.17	2/4 Oxf & Bucks LI
200173	Cpl 194	King, Leonard	Grimsbury	Banbury	115 Merton St	KIA	F+F	16.8.17	1/4 Oxf & Bucks LI
70650	Pte 195	Knight, George Edward, MM	Banbury	Oxford	29 Church Passage	DOW	F+F	9.4.18	RFA
8922	Pte 196	Leadbeater, George Henry	Banbury	-	Merton St	D	Italy	20.6.19	9 R Warwick Regt.
200550	Cpl 197	Lewis, Tom	Warwicks	Oxford	66 Causeway	D	Home	27.10.18	4 Oxf & Bucks LI
8123	L/Cpl 198	Lewis, William Henry	Leamington	Evesham	66 Causeway	KIA	F+F	18.8.17	4 Worcester Regt.
-	2 Lt 199	Lidsey, William John	-	-	Hardwick	DOW	F+F	22.3.17	RFC (16 Sqdn)
29347	Pte 200	Letherbarrow, Arthur Amos	-	-	24 Bath Terrace	DOW	F+F	8.4.18	3 Grenadier Guards
S/10794	A/Cpl 201	Lovell, Percy Frank	Banbury	Watford	19 East Street	KIA	F+F	15.9.16	9 Rifle Brigade
32733	Sgt 202	Lovell, William Ernest	Banbury	Oxford	19 East Street	KIA	F+F	9.10.16	6 Oxf & Bucks LI
-	2Lt 203	Mander, Thomas James	-	-	Bridge House, Bridge Street	D	Mespotamia	9.11.18	RE Indian Army Res
281983	Pnr 204	Makepeace, Ernest Thackery	Banbury	Banbury	14 Castle St East	D	Home	23.12.17	RE
108083	Pte 205	Mander, Norman	Grimsbury	Banbury	Bridge House, Bridge Street	KIA	F+F	11.10.17	MGC
J59239	AB 206	Mariss, James Albert	-	-	51 Queen Street	D	Home	11.1.18	RN (Vivid)
200609	Cpl 207	Marrison, Charles Henry	Grimsbury	Oxford	35 East St	KIA	Italy	15.6.18	1/4 Oxf & Bucks LI
11224	Pte 208	Matthews, William T	Kings Sutton	Banbury	-	KIA	F+F	16.5.15	2 Oxf & Bucks LI
28760	Pte 209	Maycock, Horace Herbert	-	-	127 Causeway	D	Home	26.11.18	Hampshire Regt.
R/428	Sgt/Cpl 210	McCarthy, William	London	Birmingham	35 Broughton Rd	KIA	F+F	11.10.17	8 KR R Corps
24154	Pte 211	Miller, Alfred Fredk William	Sussex	Coventry	4 Paradise Sq	KIA	F+F	9.10.17	11 R Warwick Regt.
202132	Pte 212	Minns, H W	Abingdon	Oxford	-	KIA	F+F	3.5.17	5 Oxf & Bucks LI
574642	Pte 213	Mitcalfe, Edgar Percy	Banbury	Banbury	Cornhill	KIA	EEF	2.5.18	17 London Regt.
16460	Pte 214	Mobbs, George Albert	Bermondsey	Oxford	Warwick Rd	KIA	F+F	1.7.16	1 Hampshire Regt.
1739	Pte/Cpl 215	Mobbs, William Francis	Banbury	Banbury	41 Calthorpe St	DOW	F+F	30.7.16	5th Mid Div Cyclist Comp.
209368	Dvr 216	Mobley, George Henry	-	Banbury	114 Middleton Rd	KIA	F+F	27.5.18	RE 15 Fld Coy
200605	Cpl 217	Mold, John Hartin	Neithrop	Oxford	Warwick Rd	KIA	F+F	16.8.17	1/4 Oxf & Bucks LI
96063	Pte 218	Moore, Wilfred Oswald	Banbury	Banbury	37A Queen St	KIA	F+F	29.7.17	R Sussex Regt.
18399	Pte 219	Moss, Wilfred Arthur	Banbury	Banbury	Causeway	KIA	F+F	30.7.16	2 Oxf & Bucks LI
17739	Pte 220	Munday, Ernest Arthur George	Holloway, Middx	Banbury	Islington, Middx	KIA	F+F	5.7.17	Coldstream Guards
22723	L/Cpl 221	Needham, Charles Fredk	Rutland	Banbury	21 Gatteridge St	D	F+F	2.12.17	2 Oxf & Bucks LI
17857	Pte 222	Neville, James	Gt Bourton	Oxford	9 Britannia Terrace	KIA	F+F	25.9.15	2 Oxf & Bucks LI
200610	Pte 223	Nicholls, George	Bodicote	Oxford	13 Cherwell Terrace	KIA	F+F	13.8.16	1/4 Oxf & Bucks LI
129882	Pte 224	North, Richard Jeffs	Fenny Compton	Banbury	46 East St	KIA	F+F	27.9.18	MGC
201600	Pte 225	Nutt, Percy Arthur	-	Oxford	13 Boxhedge Sq	KIA	F+F	16.8.17	1/4 Oxf & Bucks LI
9987	Pte 226	Paintin, Frank	Banbury	Banbury	20 1/2 Monument St	KIA	F+F	25.9.15	2 Oxf & Bucks LI
J33137c	Boy Teleg 227	Parker, Charles Tom Edward	-	-	32 South Bar	KIA	Jutland	31.5.16	RN HMS Black Prince
32712	Pte 228	Pearson, Charles George	Banbury	Banbury	11 Cherwell St	KIA	F+F	4.4.18	5 Oxf & Bucks LI
494807	L/Cpl 229	Pearson, Charles Williams	Banbury	Oxford	40 Britannia Rd	KIA	F+F	31.7.18	RE (479 Fld Coy)
200171	L/Cpl 230	Pearson, Martin Guy	Chipping Norton	Banbury	London City + Midland Bank	KIA	F+F	3.5.17	5 Oxf & Bucks LI
3/9280	Pte 231	Pearson, William Alfred	Eydon	Northampton	11 Cherwell St	KIA	F+F	15.12.14	2 Northampton Regt.
106503	Pte 232	Pell, William Samuel	Pitsford, Northants	Banbury	37 Southam Rd	*D	F+F	15.6.17	Labour Corps
17253	Pte 233	Perrin, Eli	Banbury	Banbury	48 Castle St West	KIA	Gallipoli	6.8.15	2 Hampshire Regt.
-	Pte 234	Phipps, Ellis J	-	-	38 Causeway	D	Home	15.9.15	Oxf & Bucks LI
33268	Pte 235	Phipps, Harry	Banbury	Woolwich	38 Causeway	KIA	F+F	1.3.17	6 Oxf & Bucks LI
2599	Pte 236	Plester, William Herbert	Grimsbury	Oxford	12 Albert St	KIA	F+F	19.7.16	1/4 Oxf & Bucks LI
89405	Pte 237	Powell, Frank	Banbury	Banbury	24 Middleton Rd	KIA	F+F	3.8.17	MGC
56312	Pte 238	Powell, John Henry	Banbury	Oxford	4 Horsefair	KIA	F+F	26.4.17	Devonshire Regt.
5824	Pte 239	Powell, William	Banbury	Banbury	29 Centre St	KIA	F+F	16.9.16	23 London Regt.
8793	L/Cpl 240	Prentice Frederick	Neithrop	Banbury	14 Townsend	D	Persian Gulf	24.10.15	1 Oxf & Bucks LI
19450	Pte 241	Prentice, William	Banbury	Oxford	Jubilee Sq, Neithrop	KIA	F+F	23.1.16	5 Oxf & Bucks LI
267599	L/Cpl 242	Prentice, Walter	Banbury	-	-	DOW	Home	-	Oxf & Bucks LI
7654	Sgt 243	Prescott, Harold	Neithrop	Banbury	22 Windsor Street	KIA	F+F	25.9.15	5 Oxf & Bucks LI
37325	Pte 244	Prescott, William Henry	Banbury	Banbury	4 Jubilee Terrace	KIA	F+F	17.4.18	1/5 DCLI
45648	Pte 245	Prickett, Louis William	Banbury	Banbury	16 Old Grimsbury Rd	DOW	F+F	11.9.18	8 R Berks Regt.
265458	L/Cpl 246	Pulker, George	Banbury	Aylesbury	3 Castle St	KIA	F+F	9.3.17	1/1 Bucks Bn Oxf & Bucks LI
19470	Pte 247	Prue, Mark Edward	Gt Bourton	Oxford	-	KIA	Persian Gulf	6.4.16	1 Oxf & Bucks LI
10663	Cpl 248	Prentice, Arthur, DCM	Banbury	Nuneaton	-	DOW	F+F	27.11.17	6 Oxf & Bucks LI
209114	Cpl 249	Prickett, E	-	-	-	DOW	Home	-	KRRC
-	Lt 250	Rathbone, George Powell	-	-	The Green	KIA	F+F	21.3.18	7 Northampshire Regt.
29455	Pte 251	Rattley, Jeffrey James	Lt Bourton	Banbury	28 Parsons St	D	Germany	4.9.18	6 Somerset LI
3425	Pte 252	Rawlings, Albert	Croughton	Manchester	Green Lane, Neithrop	DOW	At sea	10.9.15	11 Manchester Regt.
32808	Pte 253	Roberts, William George Greenway	Kineton	Oxford	24 Old Grimsbury Rd	KIA	F+F	20.2.17	QOOH
200539	Cpl 254	Robinson, Fred	Neithrop	Oxford	24 Milton St	KIA	F+F	16.8.17	1/4 Oxf & Bucks LI
5563	Pte 255	Robinson, Harold	Banbury	Oxford	9 Crouch St	D	Home	21.3.16	2/4 Oxf & Bucks LI
90495	Pte 256	Robinson, Frederick	Middleton Cheney	Banbury	Compton Villa, Castle St	KIA	F+F	6.10.17	MGC
23950	Pte 257	Rowbotham, George	Neithrop	Shorncliffe	25 Cherwell St	KIA	F+F	2.12.16	MGC
17627	Pte 258	Rowland, Edwin	Tilston, Cheshire	Oxford	19 Crouch St	KIA	F+F	16.10.15	5 Oxf & Bucks LI
210340	Cpl 259	Rutter, Horace Reginald	Banbury	Oxford	20 Castle St East	KIA	F+F	22.8.17	1/6 Gloucester Regt.
68151	Pte 260	Rutter, Percy Gordon	Middleton Cheney	Banbury	20 Castle St East	KIA	F+F	13.4.18	1st Devonshire Regt.

Mrs Clara Gibbard, mother (left) and Mrs Clara Lampitt, sister
(right) behind George Gibbard's headstone in Puchevillers
British Cemetery, Somme, France during an organised trip to
the cemeteries and battlefields. Right George Gibbard as a boy.
K Northover

Number	Rank	Name	Born	Enlisted	Home Address	How Died	Where	Date	Batt/Regiment
CH1643(s)	Pte 261	Roberts, William Joseph	-	-	Masons Arms, Newland Rd	-	F+F	26.10.17	RMLI 2nd RM Batt
6524	CSM 262	Rogers, G Joseph	Banbury	Warrington	Liverpool	KIA	F+F	23.5.16	4th Liverpool Regt.
737085	Pte 263	Rogers, J	Banbury		Previously Middleton Cheney	KIA	F+F	29.4.17	Canada 85 Inf Batt
-	Capt 264	Smith-Master, Bruce Swinton, MC	-	-	South Banbury Vicarage	KIA	F+F	1.7.16	Essex Regt.
-	2Lt 265	Smith-Master, George Arthur	-	-	South Banbury Vicarage	KIA	F+F	19.8.15	6 Bedford Regt.
Staff Nurse	Sister266	Smithies, Ellen Louise			53 Bath Rd	D	Home	22.2.19	Territorial Nursing Service
-	Capt 267	Stockton, James Godfrey	-	-	-	KIA	F+F	22.8.17	4 Oxf & Bucks LI
7621	Pte 268	Salter, Alfred	Neithrop	Oxford	33 Warwick Rd	KIA	F+F	16.5.15	2 Oxf & Bucks LI
202095	Pte 269	Sandford, Frank	Banbury	Oxford	58 Centre St, Grimsbury	D	F+F	10.3.17	2/4 Oxf & Bucks LI
11282	Pte 270	Sapsford, Frederick	Epping	Warley, Essex	58 Fish St	DOW	Egypt	11.3.18	5 Connaught Rangers.
R/16611	Pte 271	Sewell, Ellis Walter	Northants	Romsey	Horse & Jockey, West Bar	DOW	F+F	18.9.16	8 KRRifle Corps
2604	Pte 272	Sharman, Tom			64 Causeway	KIA	F+F	23.5.15	1/4 Oxf & Bucks LI
22143	L/Cpl 273	Sheasby, Algernon	Fenny Compton	Banbury	95 West St	KIA	F+F	30.7.16	2 Oxf & Bucks LI
2039	Pte 274	Sheasby, Norman F	Banbury	Churn	22 Southam Rd	DOW	F+F	1.11.14	QOOH
301577	Pte 275	Shilson, Charles Sidney		London	The Gables	KIA	F+F	1.7.16	5 London Rifle Brigade
6946	Pte 276	Simmonds, William	Banbury		8 New Rd	DOW	F+F	24.3.15	2 Oxf & Bucks LI
200563	Sgt 277	Singleton, Alfred James	Crewkerne, Somerset	Oxford	Factory St	KIA	F+F	16.8.17	1/4 Oxf & Bucks LI
RMA 12475	Gnr 278	Skuce, Albert Edward			71 Causeway	KIA	F+F	26.3.18	RMA (How BDE)
R/38146	Pte 279	Smith, Charles Henry	Banbury	Banbury	64 Warwick Rd	KIA	F+F	23.9.17	12 K R R Corps
-	Pte 280	*Smith, George T			82 Causeway	-	-		Wiltshire Regt.
237427	Gnr 281	Smith, Leonard Harry	Banbury	Northampton	Merton St	DOW	F+F	7.10.18	RFA
6005	Sgt 282	Steadman, S	Birmingham	Aldershot	29 Church Passage	KIA	Gallipoli	28.4.15	4 Worcester Regt.
20204	Pte 283	Swift, Frederick William		Banbury	14 Townsend	DOW	F+F	17.4.18	1 Dorset Regt.
G11297	Pte 284	Smith, Dennis Arthur	Byfield	Mill Hill, Middx	Banbury	KIA	F+F	2.7.16	4 Middlesex Regt.
-	Cpl 285	Sole, Bernard F H	-	-	56 Bath Rd	D	Home	7.4.20	14 London Regt.
203526	Pte 286	Steggall, William Walter Godfrey		Handels	Hackney	KIA	F+F	15.5.17	1 London Regt.
5109	L/Cpl 287	Taylor, Dennis	-	Oxford	45 Calthorpe St	DOW	F+F	1.8.16	1/4 Oxf & Bucks LI
15416	Pte 288	Taylor, Edward Arthur	Bloxham	Banbury	49 Castle St West	KIA	F+F	16.9.14	2 Grenadier Guards
4705	Pte 289	Taylor, Frank	Coventry	Coventry		KIA	F+F	18.7.16	1/8 R Warwick Regt.
981	Pte 290	Taylor, Harry Arthur	Banbury	Banbury	24 Clathorpe St	D	F+F	14.12.15	1/4 Oxf & Bucks LI
8258	L/Cpl 291	Taylor, Harry	Banbury	London	20 Compton St	KIA	F+F	23.10.14	2 Border Regt.
2503	Pte 292	Taylor, Thomas Edward	Banbury	Oxford	20 Compton St	DOW	Home	6.10.16	1/4 Oxf & Bucks LI
26692	Pte 293	Taylor, Percy Alfred Frdk	Banbury	Banbury	32 Windsor St	KIA	F+F	9.4.17	5 Oxf & Bucks LI
12098	Pte 294	Taylor, Samuei	Warwick	Merthyr	9 Townsend	DOW	Home	16.8.15	2 Welsh Regt.
G/7665	Pte 295	Thompson, Henry Gordon	Sandwich	Oxford	3 Brickyard Cott, Broughton Rd	KIA	F+F	18.3.16	6 East Kent Regt.
5026	Pte 296	Thorne, Frederick	-	Oxford		KIA	F+F	14.8.16	1/4Oxf & Bucks LI
4722	Pte 297	Thornton, Frank William	-		14 Factory St	DOW	F+F	24.7.16	1/4 Oxf & Bucks LI
75489	Gnr 298	Timms, Frederick James	Aylesbury	Aylesbury	Castle St West	KIA	F+F	4.5.17	RGA
200620	Pte 299	Timms, George William	Neithrop	Oxford	24 Union St	KIA	F+F	19.7.16	1/4 Oxf & Bucks LI
110447	Gnr 300	Townsend, Harry Matthew	Gt Bourton	Banbury	Spring Cottages	D	Home	23.1.17	RGA
9681	Pte 301	Turner, Frank Edward	Banbury	Oxford	27 Factory St	KIA	F+F	26.11.14	2 Oxf & Bucks LI
200780	Pte 302	Turner, George	-	Oxford	27 Warwick Rd	KIA	F+F	23.7.16	1/4 Oxf & Bucks LI
2813	Pte 303	Turney, Harold	-		7 Broughton Road	D	Home	-.1.17	1/4 Oxf & Bucks LI
11686	Pte 304	Tustain, James Henry	Neithrop	Rugby	59 Broughton Rd	DOW	Gallipoli	11.4.16	9 R Warwick Regt.
9694	Pte 305	Tustain, Frank	-		West Bar	D	Home	6.2.20	2 Oxf & Bucks/Labour Corps
429646	Pte 306	Tustain, Fred	Banbury	Oxford	Hardwick Fields	D	Home	19.10.18	Labour Corps
P/101	Pte 307	Tyrell, Charles	Bodicote	Aldershot	Grove St	D	F+F	12.9.15	Mounted Police
10472	L/Cpl 308	Tasker, Percy Daniel	Banbury	Rugby, Warks	Wormleighton, Warks	KIA	F+F	25.9.15	5 Oxf & Bucks LI
9495	Pte 309	Tims, Bertie	Neithrop	Banbury	-	DOW	Persian Gulf	1.1.16	1 Oxf & Bucks LI
19662	Pte 310	Upton, Eli	Banbury	Oxford	25 Factory Street	DOW	F+F	25.9.15	1 Wiltshire Regt
721032	Sgt 311	Viccars, Alfred Ernest	-	Kennington	81 Causeway	KIA	EEF	27.12.17	24 London Regt.
L/6163	Sgt 312	Viggers, Cecil John, MM	Banbury	Banbury	89 Warwick Rd	KIA	F+F	12.5.16	1 East Kent Regt.
16334	Cpl 313	Viggers, Thomas	Banbury	Oxford	9 Foundry Sq	KIA	F+F	4.7.15	1 Hampshire Regt
200952	Sgt 314	Viggers, William Edwards	-	Oxford	18b Parsons St	KIA	F+F	13.7.17	2/4 Oxf & Bucks LI
9562	Sgt 315	Vince, J A			1 Gould Sq	DOW	Home	18.7.19	Labour Corps
12092	Pte 316	Vincent, Edward	Banbury	Banbury	28 Union Street	KIA	Gallipoli	28.4.15	4 Worcester Regt.
27718	Pte 317	Wagstaffe, James Henry	Banbury	Colchester	13 Crouch St	DOW	F+F	18.4.17	1 Essex Regt.
44484	Pte 318	Walker, Henry	Nechells, Birm	Banbury	20 Lower Cherwell St	KIA	F+F	25.4.18	2/5 Gloucesterhire Regt
200188	Pte 319	Walton, James Henry	Adderbury	Banbury	2 Canal St	KIA	F+F	13.8.16	1/4 Oxf & Bucks LI
15333	Pte 320	Ward, Harry	Banbury	Plymouth	7 Castle St East	D	Mesopotamia	10.3.17	R Warwick Regt
13727	Dvr 321	Warren, Edward Harold	Banbury	Oxford	Toronto, Cnda, form Albert St	KIA	F+F	22.4.15	RE (38 Field Coy)
1489	Cpl 322	Wassall, Jack George	Shifnell	Banbury	40 Centre St, Grimsbury	D	Home	14.11.16	QOOH
200542	Pte 323	Watson, George Alfred	Priors Marston	Oxford	4 Southam Road	KIA	Italy	15.6.18	1/4 Oxf & Bucks LI
-	Lt 324	Webb, Henry			78 Bath Rd	KIA	F+F	26.4.18	RGA (9 H B)
2811	Pte 325	Wheeler, John James	-	Oxford	8 Paradise Rd	DOW	F+F	24.9.15	1/4 Oxf & Bucks LI
2610	Pte 326	White, John Henry Regd	Shotswell	Oxford	East St, Grimsbury	KIA	F+F	11.4.15	1/1 Bucks Bn, O & B L I
-	Lt 327	Whitehorn, William Joseph			36 High St	KIA	Salonika, Greece	18.9.18	7 SWB
2360	Pte 328	Whitlock, Edward	Cherwell	Oxford	6 Cherwell St	KIA	F+F	22.7.15	1/1 Bucks Bn, O & B L I
201921	Pte 329	Williams, George Henry	Banbury	Oxford	Cherwell St	KIA	F+F	29.5.18	2/4 Oxf & Bucks LI
18386	Pte 330	Willis, William Ewart	Banbury	Leicester	10 Centre St, Grimsbury	KIA	F+F	21.7.16	9 Leicester Regt.
42550	Pte 331	Wills, Arthur	Banbury	Oxford	31 Cherwell St	KIA	F+F	2.11.16	2 Worcester Regt.
840933	Pte 332	Wilkinson, Fred	Penclawdd, Glam	Swansea	14 Newland Place	KIA	F+F	6.8.17	RFA
1334	Pte 333	Wilson, Arthur Frank	Banbury	Banbury	Bath Rd	DOW	F+F	27.8.18	MGC
Ply1796(S)	Pte 334	Woods, George			34 Broad St	-	F+F	6.11.17	RMLI, 2nd RM Batt
201948	Pte 335	Wootton, Percy H	Banbury	Oxford	9 Calthorpe Gardens	D	F+F	10.6.18	2/4 Oxf & Bucks LI
RMA13127(PO)	Gnr 337	Wynne, William	-	-	4 Windsor St	KIA	Jutland	31.5.16	RMA 'HMS Lion'
2449	Sgt 337	Walter, William H		Westminster	Westminster	D	Home	17.6.15	2 London Regt.
18752	Pte 338	Watts, Charles	Neithrop	Oxford	Banbury	KIA	F+F	25.9.15	5 Oxf & Bucks
6541	Pte 339	Wodhull, William Frdrk	-		Broad St	D	Home	-/11.20	Scots Guards
8954	Pte 340	Young, Alfred	Neithrop	Oxford	19 Cherwell St	D	Mesopotamia	9.7.16	1 Oxf & Bucks LI

A group of mothers, sisters and widows on an organised pilgrimage. Mrs Clara Gibbard and Clara
Lampitt back row 2nd and 3 rd from left. Note the War Graves gardener standing far left.

K Northover

THE CHURCH ARMY

President - - - - - THE RT. HON. H. PIKE PEASE, M.P.

Founder and Hon. Chief Secretary - - - PREBENDARY CARLILE, D.D.
and Rector of St. Mary at Hill, London, E.C.

Hon. Treasurers: COL. THE RIGHT HON. SIR ARTHUR GRIFFITH-BOSCAWEN, M.P.,
Mr. F. M. ELGOOD, O.B.E.

Cheques and Postal Orders should be
drawn 'Barclay's, a/c Church
Army,' payable to PREBENDARY
CARLILE, D.D., Founder and Hon.
Chief Secretary.

*Treasury Notes should always be
sent by registered letter.*

Headquarters BRYANSTON STREET, MARBLE ARCH, LONDON, W.1.
Telegrams: "Battleaxe, Baker, London." *Telephone:* 3440 Paddington (*Four Lines—all Depts.*).

Please reply to :-

HON: SECRETARY

WAR GRAVES DEPARTMENT.

R/F

And quote reference number _____

18th Sept, 1922.

Mrs. C. Gibbard,
32, Foundry Square,
Neithrop, Banbury.

Dear Madam,

We are in receipt of your letter and note that you are
desirous of paying another visit to Puchevillers, we could
include you with a party going out on October 10th but fear
that unless we have unexpected cancellations this is the
earliest date we can offer you.

We now make Albert the Centre instead of Amiens, but
apart from that, the arrangements are the same, the visits
taking three days inclusive of outward and return journeys.
The fees are now £7. 10. 0 per head from London.

A copy of this seasons Guide Pamphlet is enclosed here-
with.

Yours faithfully,

A. Bresaw

for Hon: Sec:
War Graves Dept.

Roll No	Age	Place of Burial/Commemoration
1	26	Dorian Memorial, Greece son of Rupert and Jane Mary Akers of Stockbridge, Hants
2	26	St Sever Cemetery extension, Rouen (F) son of Mrs Ada Makepeace, 14 Castle St., East, Banbury
3	22	Beauval Com Cemetery, Somme (F) son of Ada Alexander (now Make peace) 14 Castle St., East, Banbury
4	27	Arras Memorial, (F) son of Elijah and Agnes Allen, 36 Britannia Road, Banbury
5	22	Poperinghe, New Military Cemetery (B) son of the late Mr and Mrs A Ariss, 3 London Yard, Parsons St., Banbury
6	21	Aire Communal Cemetery (F) son of George and Annie Ariss, Banbury, Oxon
7	-	Loos, British Cemetery (F) son of Mrs H Armitt, 50 Calthorpe St., Banbury
8		-
9	-	Baghdad (North Gate) War Cemetery, Iraq son of William R Armitt, Calthorpe St., Banbury
10	-	Vis-En-Artois Memorial (F)
11	28	
12	20	Thiepval Memorial, Somme (F) son of William John and Emily Barton, Pynest, Clifton Rd., Parkstone, Dorset
13	27	Lapugnoy Military, Cemetery (F) son of Charles Azel Bidmead and Marion Bidmead, Long Wittenham, Abingdon, Berks
14	28	Neuville - Bourjonval, British Cemetery (F) son of George John and M A Boast, Taxal Edge, Whaley Bridge, Cheshire. Native of Holt, Norfolk
15	39	La Clytte, Military Cemetery (B) son of George Fdk and Jane Braggins, Banbury. Husband of Winifred Mary, 23 Marlborough Rd., Banbury
16	21	Ypres (Menin Gate) Memorial (B) son of Frederick Pain Bannard and Florence N A, Grosvenor Rd., Banbury
17	22	Tyne Cot Cemetery, (B) son of John Ellen Barnes, 29 West St., Grimsbury
18	17	Plymouth Memorial, Devon (GB) son of Andrew and Sarah Barnacles of 2 Railway Cottages, Steeple Claydon, Bucks
19	27	Baghdad, (North Gate) War Cemetery, Iraq son of George and Eliza Barnes, born Banbury
20	26	Thiepval Memorial, Somme (F) son of John Henry and Annie Bartlett, 74 Stanley Road, Earlsdon, Coventry Warks.
21	21	Maroeuil British Cemetery (F) son of Frederick and Sarah Ann Batts, 12$^1/_2$ South Bar, Banbury
22	24	Ypres Reservoir Cemetery (B) brother of Miss E Bearsley, 15 Beargarden Rd., Banbury
23	28	Lijssenthoek Military Cemetery (B) husband of M A Beasley, 34 Broad St., Banbury
24	32	Etaples Military Cemetery (F) son of Fred and Ann Bedlow, Banbury. Husband of Lilian Clara Bedlow, Neithrop
25	-	Potijze Chateau Wood Cemetery (B)
26	24	Ypres (Menin Gate) Memorial (B) son of Mrs Martha Kirk, 73 Merton St., Banbury
27	-	Le Trou Aid Post Cemetery, Fleurbaix (F), son of Mr & Mrs J H Blacklock
28	-	Dozinghem Military Cemetery (B) husband of Mrs Blackwell, 34 Fish St., Banbury
29	-	St Sever Cemetery Extension, Rouen (F) son of Mr and Mrs Henry Blencowe, 20 Boxhedge Sq., Banbury
30	29	Puchevillers British Cemetery, Somme (F) son of the late Tom and Charlotte Ada Blencowe, Banbury
31	21	Ypres (Menin Gate) Memorial (B) son of Mrs C A Blencowe 61 Upper Windsor St., Banbury
32	-	Ypres (Menin Gate) memorial (B) third son of Mr and Mrs Bliss, Church Lane, Banbury
33	19	Mendinghem Military Cemetery, Poperinge (B) youngest son of Mr and Mrs

		G Bliss, Church Lane, Banbury
34	-	Thiepval Memorial, Somme (F) son of Mrs R A Bliss, 22 West Bar, Banbury
35	-	Thiepval Memorial, Somme (F)
36	-	Pozieres British Cemetery, Somme (F)
37	29	Rifle House Cemetery (B) son of George and Annie Boneham, Shotteswell, Banbury
38	20	Thiepval Memorial, Somme (F) son of Edwin and Flora Bonner, High St., Adderbury, Oxon
39	-	Vieille - Chapelle, New Military Cemetery (F)
40	-	Ypres (Menin Gate) Memorial (B)
41	21	Thiepval Memorial, Somme (F) son of Harry and Emily E Boxold, 68 High St., Banbury
42	21	Duisans British Cemetery, (F) son of John and Eliza Boyles, Banbury
43	27	Ypres (Menin Gate) Memorial (B) son of Mr and Mrs George Fdk Braggins, Banbury
44	27	Mendinghem Military Cemetery, Poperinge (B) husband of Mrs Braggins, Cherwell St., Banbury
45	22	Ploegsteert Memorial (B) son of Mrs J Hoare, 56 Calthorpe St., Banbury
46	23	Merville Communal Cemetery Extension (F) son of Henry and Avery Brain, 15 Towns End, Neithrop, Banbury
47	-	Portsmouth Naval Memorial, Hampshire (GB)
48	23	Caterpillar Valley Cemetery, Somme (F) son of John and Eliza Broughton, Trafford House, West Bar, Banbury
49	20	Etaples Military Cemetery (F) son of Annie and the late George Buller, 32 North Bar, Banbury
50	-	Royal Irish Rifles Graveyard, Laventie (F) son of Mrs G Buller, 32 North Bar, Banbury
51	28	La Neuville British Cemetery, Corbie, Somme (F) husband of Olive Annie Buller, Aero Cottage, Oak Rd., Leagrave near Luton
52	28	Duisans British Cemetery (F) son of Thomas and Mary Ann Burdett of Banbury. Husband of Harriet Drakeford, formerly Burdett of Exhall, Coventry
53	34	Etaples Military Cemetery (F) son of Helen Selina Busby and the late Harry Busby, 55 High St., Banbury
54	-	Doullens Communal Cemetery Extension No1, Somme (F) son of Henry and Anne Butler, Adderbury, Oxon
55	-	Cambrai Memorial, Louverval (F)
56	-	
57	27	Tyne Cot Memorial (B) husband of Florence Pheobe Callow, Chapel Row, Souldern
58	-	Baghdad (North Gate) War Cemetery, Iraq
59	20	Abbeville Communal Cemetery Extension, Somme (F) son of George James and Emma Carter, Oxford
60	21	Tyne Cot Cemetery (B) son of William and Elizabeth Carter, 52 East St., Grimsbury
61	-	Carnoy Military Cemetery, Somme (F) husband of Mrs E M Pratt, (formerly Carter) 3 Upper Windsor St., Banbury
62	33	Awoingt British Cemetery (F) husband of Beatrice Mary Castle, 16 Bath Terrace, Banbury
63	37	Varennes Military Cemetery, Somme (F) second son of Mr E Castle, Kings Rd., Banbury
64	25	Achiet-Le-Grande Communal Cemetery Extension (F)son of William and Jesse Maria Checkley, 44 Castle St., West, Banbury
65	-	Loos Memorial (F) husband of Mrs A L Cherry, 29 Union St., Banbury (son of Mr J Cherry, Factory St., Banbury)
66	-	
67	-	Menin Road South Military Cemetery, Ypres (B)
68	-	Greenwich Cemetery, London (GB)
69	25	Quarry Cemetery (Vermelles) (F) son of Amos and Martha Clarke, 25 Foundry Square, Banbury

The author and his mother at the grave of William Batts, Maroeuil British Cemetery, near Arras, Easter 2003.

K Northover

Delville Wood Cemetery, Somme, France. Here lie 5,520 British and Commonwealth soldiers, of these 3,590 are unknown.

K Northover

70	-	Ypres Town Cemetery Extension, Menin Gate (B) son of Mr John Clarke, West St., Banbury
71	-	Tyne Cot Memorial, Zonnebeke (B)
72	28	Arras Memorial (F) son of the late William and Sarah Clements
73	27	Philosophe British Cemetery, Mazingarbe (F) son of J F and E Clutterbuck, husband of Emma, Springfield Lodge, Banbury
74	33	Nottingham General Cemetery, Nottingham (GB) son of Mrs M A and the late Mr A N Coates. Husband of Gertrude E Coates, 363 Gladstone St., Peterborough
75	-	Pozieres Memorial, Somme (F)
76	-	
77	28	Bethune Town Cemetery (F) son of Leonard and Selina Compton, 37 Factory St., Banbury
78	20	Pozieres Memorial, Somme (F) son of Frederick Richard and Mary Compton, 23 West Bar, Banbury
79	27	Poelcapelle British Cemetery (B) son of Mrs Coleman and the late Leonard Compton, 37 Factory St., Banbury
80	-	Bethune Town Cemetery (F)
81	18	Adanac Military Cemetery, Somme (F) son of Charles and Ada Cooper, 6 South Bar, Banbury
82	28	Basra Memorial, Iraq son of William Fuller Coulthard, 10 West St., Grimsbury, Banbury
83	26	Banbury Cemetery, Oxfordshire (GB) son of George and Eliza Creed, 40 Castle St., East, Banbury
84	-	Thiepval Memorial, Somme (F)
85	-	Bac-Du-Sud British Cemetery, Baillenlval (F)
86	-	Fins New British Cemetery, Sorel-Le-Grand, Somme (F)
87	-	Pozieres Memorial, Somme (F)
88	-	Arras Memorial (F) son of Mr and Mrs Drake, Mitchum, Surrey
89	26	Point-Du-Jour Military Cemetery (F) son Ernest and Susan Dale, 22 Duke St., Banbury
90	-	Essex Farm Cemetery, Boezinge, Ypres (B) second son of Mr Aubrey Davies, late of Grimsbury
91	19	Bard Cottage Cemetery (B) son of James Samuel and Henriettta Denton, Banbury
92	-	Banbury Cemetery, Oxfordshire (GB) son of James Samuel and Henrietta Denton, Banbury
93	-	Pozieres Memorial, Somme (F)
94	28	Pozieres Memorial, Somme (F)
95	21	Thiepval Memorial, Somme (F) son of Mr S Dudley, 34 Middleton Rd., Grimsbury, Banbury
96	37	Bucquoy Road, Cemetery (F) son of Mrs E M Holton, (formerly Dumbleton) 24 High St., Banbury and the late William
97	37	Heninel Communal Cemetery Extension (F) son of Marie Holton, Banbury. Husband of Nellie Dumbleton, 80 Honey Hill Rd., Bedford
98	-	Thiepval Memorial, Somme (F)
99	24	Awoingt British Cemetery (F) son of George and Ellen Dearlove, Bletchington, Oxon native of Grimsbury
100	-	St Sever Cemetery Extension, Rouen (F)
101	-	Banbury Cemetery, Oxfordshire (GB) son of Walter and Elizabeth Eaves of Banbury. Husband of Hannah, Turners Arms, Bicester
102	-	Basra Memorial, Iraq son of Mrs Job Eden, Boxhedge
103	-	Baghdad (North Gate) War Cemetery, Iraq son of Mrs Job Eden, Boxhedge
104	18	Lillers Communal Cemetery (F) son of Job and Elizabeth Eden, 9 Boxhedge Sq., Banbury
105	-	Banbury Cemetery, Oxfordshire (GB)
106	24	Rocquigny-Equancourt Road British Cemetery, Somme (F) son of Fdk and Hannah Fairfax, Causeway, Banbury. Husband of Caroline, 33 Warwick Rd., Banbury
107	42	Etaples Military Cemetery (F) brother of F L Fox, 39 Gosbrook Rd.,

Former members of the Oxfordshire and Buckinghamshire Light Infantry who revisited the battlefields of France and Flanders c1937. Back row, left to right 3 Claridge; Middle row left to right 2 J Gillett, 3 G Painting, 4 H Slaymaker, 6 Benjy Clarke. front row left to right 1 Jackson, 2 Frank Green, 3 Bob Giles, 4 Col Maurice Edmunds, 5 A A Thornitt, 6 E Coleman, 7 Tom Wynne.

K Northover

		Caversham, Reading, Berks
108	19	Arras Memorial (F) son of Mrs A Franklin, 10 Southam Rd., Banbury
109	-	La Brique Military Cemetery No 2, Ypres (B) son of Mr and Mrs Luke French, 19 Monument St., Banbury
110		Le Touret Memorial (F)
111	32	Bethune Town Cemetery (F) husband of Minnie Davey French, 5 Factory St., Banbury
112	19	Vadencourt British Cemetery (F) son of George and Eliza Ann French, 12 Bath Terrace, Banbury
113	-	
114	31	Ration Farm Military Cemetery, La Chapelle-D'Armentieres (F) son of Henry Thomas Friend, Great Tew, Enstone, Oxon and the late Mary
115	27	Eclusier Communal Cemetery, Somme (F) eldest son of Mr and Mrs F W Fell, 20 Globe Yard, Calthorpe St., Banbury
116	20	Montay-Neuvilly Road Cemetery (F) son of Charles and Sarah Bella C Ford, 51 Bridge St., Banbury
117	28	Beauval Communal Cemetery, Somme (F) son of Dr Innes Griffin and Mary Eliza of Dashwood House, Banbury
118	20	Heninel-Croisilles Road Cemetery (F) son of C W Gardiner, 66 Bridge St., Banbury
119	19	Neuville-Bourjonval British Cemetery (F) son of Roland and M E Garnett, 91 High St., Banbury
120	19	Adanac Military Cemetery, Somme (F) son of Harry W H and Margaret Gaunt, 14 Elm St, Buckingham, native of Banbury
121	20	Rosieres British Cemetery, Somme (F) son of Minnie and Thomas Gillett, 13 Duke St, Banbury
122	29	Ruyaulcourt Military Cemetery, son of Frederick and Amelia Gillett Husband of Mary E Gillet, Sibford Ferris
123	-	Peronne Communal Cemetery Extension, Ste Radegonde, Somme (F) son of Mr and Mrs James Gillett
124	22	Puchevillers British Cemetery, Somme (F), son of Edward and Clara Gibbard, 32 Foundry Sq., Banbury
125	26	Basra Memorial, Iraq, son of Edward and Clara Gibbard, 32 Foundry Sq., Banbury
126	30	Beaurains Road Cemetery, Beaurains (F), son of John and Kate Mary Gibbard: husband of Mabel Lucy Gibbard, 12 Clathorpe St. Banbury
127	-	Cambrai Memorial, Louverval, Nord (F)
128	-	Heilly Station Cemetery Mericourt-L'Abbe, Somme (F) husband of Mrs Gilkes, Birmingham, late of 35 Causeway, Banbury
129	-	Banbury Cemetery, Oxfordshire (GB)
130	26	Boscon British Cemetery (Italy) son of Miriam and William Golby of Banbury
131	-	Tyne Cot Cemetery, Zonnebeke (B) son of Mr and Mrs Green, Chiswick, London late of 5 North Bar, Banbury
132	-	Millencourt Communal Cemetery Extension, Somme (F)
133	20	Artillery Wood Cemetery (B) son of Charles and Caroline Gregory, 86 Warwick Rd, Banbury
134	19	Westhof Farm Cemetery, Heuvelland (B) son of Mr and Mrs Godfrey, North Bar, Banbury
135	-	Vis-En-Artois Memorial (F) son of Mr and Mrs Godfrey, North Bar, Banbury
136	27	Vimy Memorial (F) son of Edwin Goodwin, 21 Monument St., Banbury
137	19	Ypres (Menin Gate) Memorial (B) son of Mrs E Grimsley, 38 Church Lane and the late Mr W Grimsley
138	63	Banbury Cemetery, Oxfordshire (GB)
139	-	Ploegsteert Memorial, Hainaut (B)
140	22	Mont Huon Military Cemetery (F) son of William and Harriet Garrett of Hawksbury Stop Canal Office, Coventry
141	21	Coventry (London Road) Cemetery, Warwickshire (UK), son of George and Sylvia Garside, 47A Widdrington Rd., Coventry
142		Vis-En-Artois Memorial (F)

Roland Garnett

R Gillett

Thomas Gibbard

K Northover

143	21	Catterpillar Valley Cemetery, Somme (F) son of Mrs A L Hunt and the late John Hunt, (solicitor), 46 The Green, Banbury
144	-	Aubers Ridge, British Cemetery, Aubers (F)
145	-	Masnieres British Cemetery, Marcoing (F)
146	21	Lillers Communal Cemetery (F), son of Rose Ellen Evins (formerly Harris) and Robert Henry Evins (stepfather) 24 Crouch St
147		Epehy Wood Farm Cemetery, Epehy, Somme (F) second son of Mr and Mrs G Harris, Warwick Rd., Banbury
148	28	Niederzwehren Cemetery (G)
149	45	Thiepval Memorial, Somme, (F) son of Thomas and Hannah Harrison, Northend, Husband of Elizabeth, Rugby
150	19	Dadizele New British Cemetery (B), son of Mr G W and Mrs Clara Hartwell, 10 New Road, Banbury
151	20	Le Vertanney British Cemetery, Hinges (F), son of Mr G W and Mrs Clara Hartwell, 10 New Road, Banbury
152		Helles Memorial, Turkey
153		
154	34	Bulls Road Cemetery, Flers, Somme (F) son of Mr and Mrs Hazell, 21 Albert St., Banbury
155	20	Banbury Cemetery, Oxfordshire (GB)
156	32	Sun Quarry Cemetery (F), husband of Lizzie Heritage, 59 Queens St., Banbury
157	23	Aveluy Communal Cemetery, Somme (F), son of Arthur and Elizabeth Hirons, 4 Fish St., Banbury
158		Essex Farm Cemetery, Boezinge, Ypres (B)
159		Loos Memorial (F)
160	19	Varennes Military Cemetery, Somme (F), son of Mr C Hoare of 'Boat Caroline', Wyken Colliery, Coventry
161	37	Arras Memorial (F), son of James and Sarah Ann Hobbs, husband of Eleanore Mary Hobbs, 9 Bath Cottage, Banbury
162	19	Gorre British and Indian Cemetery (F), yougest son of Mr and Mrs James Hobbs, 28 Crouch St, Banbury
163		Portsdown (Christchurch) Military Cemetery, Hampshire (UK)
164	35	Duhallow ADS Cemetery, Ypres (B), son of William Henry & Mary Hodges, 19 Sycamore Rd, Waterloo, Liverpool
165	32	Banbury Cemetery, Oxfordshire
166		Charmes Military Cemetery, Essegney, Vosges (F)
167		Queant Road Cemetery, Buissy (F) husband of Mrs Hopkins, 98 West St., Grimsbury
168	-	Ypres (Menin Gate) Memorial (B)
169	-	Tyne Cot Memorial, Zonnebeke (B)
170	24	Thiepval Memorial, Somme (F) son of John & Kate Humphris, 83 Merton St, Banbury
171		
172	23	Thiepval Memorial, Somme (F) only son of Richard W Humphris, 25 Mitchell St., St Lukes, London
173	20	Thiepval Memorial, Somme (F), son of George and Sarah Hutchings, 43 Calthorpe St., Banbury
174	29	Vlamertinghe Military Cemetery (B), son of Frederick and Esther Hyde, Rowsley, Derbyshire. Husband of Ada Hyde, Mickleton, Gloucestershire
175	18	Le Touret Memorial (F) son of George F Huckins, 6 Southam Road Court, Banbury and the late Florence
176	28	Bancourt British Cemetery (F), son of William and Polly Hucklebridge, 5 Palmerston Rd., Taunton, Somerset
177	-	Boscon British Cemetery, Italy
178		Tyne Cot Memorial, Zonnebeke (B) son of the late Alfred Impey
179	27	Boulogne Eastern Cemetery (F)
180	20	La Ferte-Sous-Jourre Memorial (F) son of James Alfred and Mahala Jackson, 62 Kings Road, Banbury
181		Thiepval Memorial, Somme (F) youngest son of Mr and Mrs A Jarvis, Fish

Charles William Pearson

K Northover

Veterans of the Queens Own Oxfordshire Hussars on a pilgrimage to France and Flanders after the war.
Back row from left to right; Percy Batchelor (with pipe), Maurice French, sixth Harry Stroud. Front row,
Nelson Bradshaw, sixth Arthur Whitmill.

Stroud Family

		St., Banbury
182	33	Birr Cross Roads Cemetery (B), son of William Clarke Jelfs and Mary Jelfs, 48 West Bar, Banbury
183	45	Banbury Cemetery, Oxfordshire (UK), son of John and Emma Jennings, husband of Sarah Sophia 19 Gatteridge St., Banbury
184	28	Wimereux Communal Cemetery (F)
185	28	Tincourt New British Cemetery, Somme (F), son of Mr W L and Mrs A Jones, 23 Albert St., Banbury
186	19	Vis-En-Artois Memorial (F), son of Mr and Mrs T W Jordan, 5 Grove St., Banbury
187	-	Ypres (Menin Gate) Memorial (B)
188	29	Etaples Military Cemetery (F). Killed by enemy aircraft, son of William and Lucy Jones, husband of N H Jones, 19 Compton St., Banbury
189	24	Arras Memorial (F) son of Mrs Kennedy and the late Mr William Kennedy, 50 Centre St., Banbury
190	-	Hargicourt Communal Cemetery Extension, Aisne (F) husband of Mrs King, North St., Grimsbury
191	17	Thiepval Memorial, Somme, son of Mrs C E Bidmead, 4 Cherwell St., Banbury
192	44	New Irish Farm Cemetery (B) husband of Alice H Faithorn (formerly Kilby) 57 Kings Road, Banbury
193	20	Thiepval Memorial, Somme (F) youngest son of Pc Kilby and Mrs Kilby, County Police Station, Banbury
194	24	Tyne Cot Memorial, Zonnebeke (B), son of Sarah Ann King,115 Merton St., Banbury and the late Tom King
195	-	Ploegsteert Memorial (B)
196	27	Faenza Community Cemetery, Italy, son of Sarah E Gammon (formerly Leadbeater) of Worcester and the late John Henry
197	27	Banbury Cemetery, Oxfordshire (GB) son of Mr and Mrs T Lewis, 66 The Causeway, Banbury
198	-	Artillery Wood Cemetery, Boesinghe (B) son of Mr and Mrs T Lewis, 66 The Causeway, Banbury
199	21	Aubigny Communal Cemetery Extension (F), son of William Isaac Richard and Emily Crosier Lidsey of Banbury
200	29	Gezaincourt Communal Cemetery Extension, Somme, eldest son of the late Arthur and Elizabeth Letherbarrow of Banbury
201	20	Thiepval Memorial, Somme (F), son of Benjamin and Charlotte Agnes Lovell, 19 East St., Grimsbury, Banbury
202	25	Thiepval Memorial, Somme (F) son of Benjamin and Charlotte Agnes Lovell, 19 East St., Grimsbury, Banbury
203	-	Tehran War Cemetery, Iran son of Mrs E Mander, late of Bridge House, Bridge St., Banbury
204		Banbury Cemetery, Oxfordshire (UK)
205	24	Tyne Cot Memorial (B), son of Emilia Mander, 5 Springfield Avenue, Banbury and the late Mr J T Mander
206	20	Staines (London Road) Cemetery, Middlesex (UK), son of Mr T H and Mrs M E Marris, 38 High St., Staines
207	26	Boscon British Cemetery, Italy, son of Henry & Clara Marrison of Grimsbury, Banbury
208	22	Le Touret Memorial (F), only son of William and Ann Matthews, Wales St., Station Rd., Kings Sutton
209	19	Banbury Cemetery, Oxfordshire (UK), youngest son of Sarah Ann Maycock of 127 Causeway, Banbury and the late Stephen Maycock
210	-	Oxford Road, Cemetery, Ypres (B)
211	28	Tyne Cot Memorial (B), son of Alfred James and Matilda Miller of 1 Paradise Sq, Bath Rd, Banbury
212	22	Arras Memorial (F), son of Mrs P W Minns of Wootton, Berks
213	20	Jerusalem Memorial (Israel), son of Leonard Mitcalfe of Cornhill Mansion, Banbury and the late Minna Gregor Mitcalfe
214	32	Thiepval Memorial, Somme (F), son of James Charles Robert and Clara

The Thiepval Memorial to the missing on the Somme. Carved on stone panels are the names of 73,357 British and South African soldiers who died in the battles of 1916-17, who have no known grave.

K Northover

Tyne Cot Cemetery, Zonnebeke, West Flanders, Belgium. The cemetery contains 11,908 graves, the greatest number to be buried in any Commonwealth War Cemetery.

K Northover

		Esther Mobbs
215	19	Boulogne Eastern Cemetery, son of Thomas and Kate Elizabeth Mobbs, 41 Calthorpe St., Banbury
216	-	Soissons Memorial, Aisne (F)
217	24	Tyne Cot Memorial (B) son of Thomas William and Mary Elizabeth Mold, 3 Finlay Terrace, Warwick Rd., Banbury
218	22	Monchy British Cemetery (F), son of Mr and Mrs W B Moore, 37a Queen St., Banbury
219	23	Thiepval Memorial, Somme (F), son of W W T Moss
220		Artillery Wood Cemetery, Boezinge, Ypres (B)
221	27	Rocquigny-Equancourt Rd., British Cemetery, Somme (F), son of F E Needham, Culworth; husband of Beatrice M Needham 21 Gatteridge St., Banbury
222	29	Loos Memorial (F) son of George and Hannah Neville, Gt Bourton. Husband of Ada Mary Neville 9 Britannia Terrace, Banbury
223	22	Thiepval Memorial, Somme (F), son of Mrs E Nicholls, 13 Cherwell Terrace, Banbury
224	19	Vadencourt British Cemetery (F), son of William John and Zilpah North, 46 East Street, Grimsbury, Banbury
225	-	Tyne Cot Memorial, Zonnebeke (B)
226	23	Loos Memorial (F), son of Mrs Kate Paintin of $20^1/_2$ Monument Street, Banbury
227	17	Chatham Memorial, Kent (GB) son of Mr and Mrs C E Parker 32 South Bar, Banbury
228	20	Beacon Cemetery, Somme, son of Charles and Ada Pearson 11 Cherwell Street, Banbury
229	22	Les Baraques Military Cemetery, Sangette (F), son of Louisa & John Jackson (Stepfather) 40 Britannia Road, Banbury
230	-	Arras Memorial (F), son of Mr M K Pearson, Chipping Norton
231	19	Le Touret Memorial (F) son of Charles and Ada Pearson 11 Cherwell Street, Banbury
232	36	Reninghelst New Military Cemetery (B) son of Mr and Mrs Pell, husband of E A Pell, 27 Southam Road, Banbury
233	-	Helles Memorial, Turkey (G)
234	-	-
235	19	Thiepval Memorial, Somme (F), son of William and Elizabeth Phipps, 38 Causeway, Grimsbury, Banbury
236	30	Thiepval Memorial, Somme (F), son of William Plester
237	34	Ypres (Menin Gate) Memorial (B) son of Frederick and Eliza E Powell
238	41	Arras Memorial (F) brother of Mrs H A Beard, 4 Horsefair, Banbury
239	29	Thiepval Memorial, Somme (F), son of the late Job and Mary Powell, husband of Agnes Mary 48 Middleton Road, Banbury
240	26	Basra War Cemetery, Iraq, son of William and Emma Prentice, Neithrop, Banbury
241	32	Talana Farm Cemetery, Ypres (B), husband of Mrs Prentice, Jubilee Terrace, Banbury
242	-	
243	-	Ypres (Menin Gate) Memorial (B)
244	19	Loos Memorial (F), son of Mr and Mrs A Prescott, 4 Jubilee Terrace, Banbury
245	-	St Sever Cemetery Extension, Rouen (F)
246	30	Hem Farm Military Cemetery, Somme, son of George and Sarah Pulker, 28 Albert Street, Banbury
247	-	Basra Memorial, Iraq
248	24	Tincourt New British Cemetery, Somme (F), son of William and Emma Prentice, Neithrop, Banbury
249	-	Butlers Marston (SS Peter and Paul) Churchyard, Warks (GB)
250	29	Pozieres Memorial, Somme (F) second son of Mr and Mrs F Rathbone, Butchers Row, Banbury
251	19	Niederzwehren Cemetery, Germany, son of James and Florence Rattley, 28 Parsons Street, Banbury

252	-	Helles Memorial, Turkey (Gallipoli)
253	21	Thiepval Memorial, Somme (F), son of George and Winifred Roberts, 24 Old Grimsbury Road, Banbury
254	32	Tyne Cot Memorial (B), son of Daniel and Anne Robinson, 24 Milton Street, Banbury
255	23	Banbury Cemetery, Oxfordshire (GB), youngest son of Daniel Robinson, 9 Crouch Street, Banbury
256	33	Tynecot Memorial (B), son of James Robinson, Three Tuns Inn, Cherwell Banbury. Husband of Lilian Brown (form Robinson), St Giles, Salisbury
257	26	Thiepval Memorial, Somme (F) son of George Bryan and Hannah Rowbotham, 25 Cherwell Street, Banbury
258	18	Menin Gate Memorial (B) , son of Sarah Rowlands and the late William Rowlands, 19 Crouch Street, Banbury
259	19	New Irish Farm Cemetery (B) son of William H and Fanny M Rutter, 20 Castle Street East, Banbury
260	19	Aval Wood Military Cemetery, Vieux-Berquin (F) son of William H and Fanny M Rutter, 20 Castle St., East, Banbury
261	-	Passschendaele New British Cmetery, Zonnebeke, (B)
262	-	Cambrin Military Cemetery (F)
263	-	La Chaudiere Military Cemetery, Vimy (F)
264	24	Sucrerie Military Cemetery, Colincamps, Somme (F), son of John Ernest and Eliza Margaret Smith-Masters, Warren Lodge, Newberry, native of Kidmore End, Oxon
265	20	Dranoutre Military Cemetery, West Vlaanderen (B) son of John Ernest and Eliza Margaret Smith-Masters of Caner Meopham, Kent
266	42	City of London Cemetery, Essex (GB) daughter of A H and Henrietta M Smithies of 245 York Road, West Hartlepool. Born London
267	25	Tyne Cot memorial, Zonnebeke (B) eldest son of Mrs Stockton, Falmouth and the late O J Stockton, Banbury
268	28	Le Touret Memorial, (F) son of Harry and Emily Salter 33 Warwick Road, Banbury
269	-	Cerisy-Gailly Military Cemetery, Somme (F)
270	28	Ramleh War Cemetery, Israel son of Frederick and Mary Sapsford, husband of Florence Amy 58 Fish Street, Banbury
271	24	Heilly Station Cemetery, Merricourt-L'Abbe, Somme sonof Harry and Annie Sewell, 46 Queens Road, Banbury
272	-	Rifle House Cemetery, Hainaut (B)
273	19	Thiepval Memorial, Somme (F) son of John William and Fanny Sheasby, 95 West Street, Grimsbury, Banbury
274	21	Longuenesse (St Omer) Souvenier Cemetery (F) son of Edward Joseph and Mary Ann Sheasby, 8 Castle Street West, Banbury
275	26	Thiepval Memorial, Somme (F) son of Edith Shilson, Gables, Banbury and the late Charles Johnson Shilson
276	-	Bethune Town Cemetery (F)
277	28	Tyne Cot Memorial (B) son of Samuel and Elizabeth Singleton, 15 Factory Street, Banbury
278	-	Faubourg-D'Amiens Cemetery, Arras (F)
279	-	Cement House Cemetery, Langemark (B)
280		
281	-	Vis-En-Artois Memorial (F) son of Mr and Mrs S D Smith, Merton Street, Banbury
282	-	Redoubt Cemetery, Helles, Turkey (Gallipoli)
283	19	Ste Marie Cemetery, Le Havre (F) son of John Henry and Anne Swift, Neithrop, Banbury
284	19	Thiepval Memorial, Somme (F) son of Jabez and Sarah-Anne Smith, 2 Boxhedge Lane, Banbury
285		
286	19	Arras Memorial (F) eldest son of Mrs A Truelock, Yew Tree House, Bodicote, nr Banbury
287	-	Heilly Station Cemetery, Merricourt-L'Abbe, Somme (F) son of Mr and Mrs

Charles Marrison

K Northover

The Menin Gate Memorial to the missing, Ypres. The memorial is situated on the eastern side of the town of Ypres, West Flanders, Belgium. It bears the names of 54,896 soldiers who were lost without trace during the defence of the salient between 1914 and 1917.

K Northover

		Frederick Taylor, Calthorpe Street, Banbury
288	24	La Ferte-Sous-Jouarre Memorial (F) son of the late George William and Margaret Esther Taylor
289	19	Thiepval Memorial, Somme (F)
290	25	Villers-Bosage Communal Cemetery, Somme (F) son of Henry and Emily Taylor, Banbury
291	27	Menin Gate Memorial son of John and Ann S M P Taylor, 20 Compton Street, Banbury
292	20	Banbury Cemetery, Oxfordshire son of John and Ann S M P Taylor, 20 Compton Street, Banbury
293	-	Tilloy British Cemetery, Tilloy-Les-Mofflaines (F)
294	-	Kensal Green, (All Souls) Cemetery, London son of Thomas and Charlotte Taylor
295	-	Loos Memorial (F) husband of Mrs Thompson
296	-	Thiepval Memorial (F)
297	19	Warloy-Baillon Community Cemetery Extension, Somme son of Arthur Eli and Emily Thornton born at Banbury
298	32	Mindel Trench British Cemetery, St Laurent-Blangy (F) husband of Ethel E Timms, 50 Castle Street West, Banbury
299	30	Thiepval Memorial, Somme (F) son of Reuben and Fanny Timms, Middleton Cheney, husband of Rhoda Timms, 24 Union Street, Banbury
300	-	Cropredy (St Marys) Churchyard, Oxfordshire husband of Florence L Townsend, Kentish Cottage, Cropredy
301	-	Ypres (Menin Gate) Memorial (B)
302	-	Thiepval Memorial, Somme (F)
303	22	Banbury Cemetery, Oxfordshire (GB)
304	-	Amara War Cemetery, Iraq
305	-	
306	25	Oxford (Botley) Cemetery, Oxfordshire, youngest son of Benjamin Tustain of Hardwick Fields, Banbury
307	50	Merville Communal Cemetery Extension (F) husband of Mary Ellen Tyrell of 25 The Bourne, Hook Norton
308	29	Ypres (Menin Gate) Memorial son of Caroline Hawkins (formerly Tasker) and the late Timothy of Wormleighton, Leamington Spa
309	-	Kut War Cemetery, Iraq
310	-	Lijssenthoek Military Cemetery (B) father of Mr W Upton, 25 Factory Street, Banbury
311	27	Jerusalem War Cemetery son of Joseph and Hannah Viccars, Banbury, husband of Clara Viccars, Banbury
312	36	Essex Farm Cemetery (B) son of John H and A M Viggars, 89 Warwick Road, Banbury
313	-	Ypres (Menin Gate) Memorial (B) husband of Mrs Viggers, 9 Foundry Square, Banbury
314	22	Tyne Cot Memorial (B) son of Mrs Alice Viggers, 18b London Yard, Parsons Street, Banbury
315	50	Banbury Cemetery, Oxfordshire husband of S A Vince 14 St Georges Crescent, Banbury
316	23	Helles Memorial (G) son of Mrs Mary Vincent, 28 Union Street, Banbury
317	32	Douai Community Cemetery (F) son of John and Harriet Wagstaff, 13 Crouch Street, Banbury
318	18	Loos Memorial (F) son of James and Trezah Walker, 20 Lower Cherwell Street, Banbury
319	-	London Cemetery and Extension, Longueval, Somme (F)
320	40	Basra Memorial, Iraq son of Mr Ward, Banbury, husband of Elizabeth Ward, 59 Edward Street, Redditch, Worcestershire
321	27	New Irish Farm Cemetery (B) son of Emily Louisa Collinge (formerly Warren) 3 Easthill, Colchester, and the late Mr Warren native of Banbury
322	28	Banbury Cemetery, Oxfordshire son of Arthur G Wassell, 40 Centre Street, Grimsbury, Banbury
323	25	Boscon British Cemetery (Italy) son of Ellen Watson, Banbury

324	32	Duhallow ADS Cemetery, Ypres (B) son of Mary Webb of Higham Ferrers, Northants and the late William Webb husband of Gertrude Webb,132 Beaconsfield Road, Leicester
325	22	Louvencourt Military Cemetery, Somme son of John Day and Rachel Wheeler 8 Paradise Road, Banbury
326	19	Lancashire Cottage Cemetery (B) son of Thomas Henry and Sarah Emma White, 10 Old Grimsbury Road, Banbury
327	36	Dorian Memorial, Greece son of the late William Lampet Whitehorn and Betsy Whitehorn, 36 High Street, Banbury
328	-	Gommecourt Wood New Cemetery, Foncquevillers (F)
329	19	St Venat-Robecq Road British Cemetery (F) son of George Williams, Banbury
330	21	Thiepval Memorial, Somme (F) son of Samuel and Emma Willis, 10 Centre Street, Banbury
331	-	Thiepval Anglo-French Cemetery, Somme (F)
332		Kline-Vierstraat British Cemetery, Kemmel (B)
333	19	Ligny-St-Flochel British Cemetery, Averdoingt (F) son of the late Frank and Emma Wilson
334	21	Tyne Cot Memorial (B) son of Edmund and Kate Woods, 34 Broad Street, Banbury
335	-	Niederzwheren Cemetery, Germany
336	21	Portsmouth Naval Memorial (GB) son of Annie Hirons (formerly Wynne) 4 Windsor Terrace, Banbury and the late Thomas Frederick Wynne
337	45	Kensal Green (All Souls) Cemetery, London (GB) husband of E B Walters of 36 Ockendon Road, Essex Road, Islington, London
338	32	Ypres (Menin Gate) Memorial (B) husband of Louisa Watts, 7 New Houses, Bodicote, Banbury
339	32	Banbury Cemetery, Oxfordshire
340	-	Basra Memorial, Iraq

✱Notes to the Banbury Roll of Honour

✻ George Armitt
This seems to be a duplication as his name appears on the Roll under the Oxford & Bucks LI and the London Regiment sections. He enlisted into the the 1st/4th Oxford & Bucks LI with the regimental number 1746. At some point he transferred to the 12th Battalion London Regiment (The Rangers) and was killed in action whilst serving with that unit.

✻W G Caisbrook
A resident of 70 Merton Street and known to be serving as a gunner in the Royal Horse Artillery in September 1915. No trace of medal entitlement has been found therefore it seems he had no service overseas. He is not listed by the Commonwealth War Graves Commission so it is assumed he did not die while serving in the armed forces.

✻ R Cherry
Only one R Cherry can be traced as a casualty with the Oxford & Bucks LI, that of 9227 Pte Richard Cherry, 'missing believed killed after the battle of Loos.' It is therefore possible that they are the same person. The *Banbury Guardian* of July 27, 1916 reports: 'Pte R Cherry of the Oxford & Bucks LI, son of Mr J Cherry, Factory Street is reported killed.

✻ Leonard J Compton

Born circa 1890 in Banbury. Worked pre-war at the Lucas Linen factory and played football for the works team as well as for Banbury Juniors FC during the 1909 season. A pre war territorial, no 1875 (renumbered 200234 in 1917) he served in C Company 1st/4th Oxford & Bucks LI throughout the war. No trace of death can be located. His father, Leonard J C Compton died at Factory Street on February 22, 1915 aged 58 but no evidence of military service has been found.

✻ George Henry Humphris

Recorded as having lived at 12 Lower Windsor Street in another, printed, Banbury Roll of Honour. It is thought that he is one and the same person in George Henry Williams. In the *Banbury Guardian* June 20, 1918 it states: 'Mrs Humphris 12 Lower Windsor Street has received official news that her grandson, Pte G H Williams was killed in action on May 29, 1918.

✻ George T Smith

Fifteen men of this name are listed as casualties by the Commonwealth Wargraves Commission. None are listed from the Wiltshire Regiment, neither can any be positively identified as being connected with Banbury.

The unknown soldier, a snapshot of a British soldier lying in an abandoned trench. The photograph believed to have been taken by a German soldier was developed and printed by an enterprising photographic company in Belgium. The caption on the reverse merely reads 'Somme casualty'.

K Northover

Roll of Honour key to abbreviations

2Lt	=	Second Lieutenant
A/	=	Acting Rank
AB	=	Able Seaman
A&S	=	Argyll & Sutherland
ADJ	=	Adjutant
ASC	=	Army Service Corps
AVC	=	Army Veterinary Corps
(B)	=	Belgium
Batt	=	Battalion or Battery
Berks	=	Berkshire
Bglr	=	Bugler
Bn	=	Battalion
Boy 1	=	Boy 1st Class
C	=	Corps
Capt	=	Captain
Coronel	=	Naval battle
Coy	=	Company
Cpl	=	Corporal
CSM	=	Company Sergeant Major
D	=	Died of illness (or wounds caused by service)
DCLI	=	Duke of Cornwall L I
DoD	=	Died of Disease
DoW	=	Died of Wounds
DVR	=	Driver
EEF	=	Egyptian Expeditionery Force
(F)	=	France
F/F	=	France/Flanders, ie Western Front
Fld	=	Field
G	=	Germany
GL	=	General list
Gnr	=	Gunner
Grp	=	Group
HB	=	Heavy Battery
HLI	=	Highland Light Infantry
Home	=	United Kingdom
How Bde	=	Howitzer Brigade

Inf	=	Infantry
Innisk	=	Inniskilling
Jutland	=	Naval Battle
KIA	=	Killed in Action
KRRC	=	Kings Royal Rifle Corps
Lab	=	Labour
L/Cpl	=	Lance Corporal
LI	=	Light Infantry
Lt	=	Lieutenant
MGC	=	Machine Gun Corps
MT	=	Mechanised Transport
OHB	=	Oxfordshire Heavy Battery
Oxf & Bucks LI	=	Oxford & Bucks Light Infantry
Pnr	=	Pioneer
Pte	=	Private
QOOH	=	Queens Own Oxfordshire Hussars
RAF	=	Royal Air Force
RAMC	=	Royal Army Medical Corps
RASC	=	Royal Army Service Corps
RE	=	Royal Engineers
Res	=	Reserve
RFA	=	Royal Field Artillery
RFC	=	Royal Flying Corps
Rfn	=	Rifleman
RGA	=	Royal Garrison Artillery
RHA	=	Royal Horse Artillery
RM	=	Royal Marines
RMA	=	Royal Marine Artillery
RMLI	=	Royal Marine Light Infantry
RN	=	Royal Navy
RND	=	Royal Naval Division
Sect	=	Section
SGT	=	Sergeant
SPR	=	Sapper
SQDN	=	Squadron

Stat Hosp	=	Stationary Hospital
Sth Mid Div	=	South Midland Division
Teleg	=	Telegraphist
Yeo	=	Yeomanry
/	=	Previous or later unit

"In the officers' quarters you'll be expected to get up at four, clean out the mess, do as you're told, and no back answers!"

"It's a gift, sir!— I've been married twenty years!"

Bamforth comic card sent to a Mrs T Drake of Marlborough Road in March 1917. It refers to the conscription of married men, begun some ten months earlier.

K Northover

The annual Remembrance Day Service and parade through the town in November 1980
Bill Simpson

The head of the parade lead by the St John Ambulance Brigade Band arriving at Bridge Street from Broad Street

Bill Simpson